COURT OF INQUIRY

COURT OF INQUIRY

"Neglecting the Possible" — U.S. Navy Mistakes

by

Benjamin S. Persons

SUNFLOWER UNIVERSITY PRESS®

1531 Yuma • P.O. Box 1009 • Manhattan, Kansas 66505-1009 USA

Photos: U.S. Navy Archives

ISBN 0-89745-256-9

Sunflower University Press is a wholly-owned subsidiary
of the non-profit 501(c)3 Journal of the West, Inc.

For Ben S. Persons, who I never knew,
John Howard Neisler, my friend,
my fraternity brother, and my mentor,
and for his daughter Frances who has borne my children.

Contents

Acknowledgment

*F*ORMER Lieutenant (Junior Grade) Vance O. Rankin III, who served on the USS *Bache* and is now an attorney in Atlanta, inspired this book. When it was thought the work would only encompass the life and death of the *Bache*, I urged Rankin to be a co-author of the story. Perhaps the power of persuasion was insufficient, for this did not come to be. However, Rankin was a trusted adviser on naval matters and, in particular, on the strange fate of his former ship. His inspiration and counsel were the necessary elements, and for this he is thanked.

Ben Persons
Atlanta, 2001

Preface

THE COURT of Inquiry is an investigative body of the U.S. Navy, the U.S. Army, or the U.S. Air Force, authorized to invoke the hearing procedure and to reach a conclusion as to the facts surrounding a major incident. The Court of Inquiry is analogous to a Grand Jury that hears witnesses, sifts the data disclosed, and determines if that which has been heard warrants a "True-Bill," or indictment, which would result in a formal trial. Almost without exception, the result of a Court of Inquiry either has been exoneration and dismissal of charges or a fixing of probable culpability, resulting in a general court-martial.

The U.S. Navy has defined "major incidents" as reasons for investigation, but that definition is not all-inclusive nor is it always followed. Most significant is the matter of public opinion. If it is believed that the public is aroused over a happening such as the sinking of a ship or the killing of friendly sailors or civilians by U.S. Navy actions, then a Court of Inquiry is convened. If it is believed that not much will come of the incident, then the Navy will quietly put the matter behind itself, to avoid showing its "dirty linen."

During wartime, incidents frequently happen, which were they to occur during peacetime would result in a court-martial. Yet not so in war. It is not always well to expose the system to scrutiny. If the public had no knowledge of the sinking of the cruiser USS *Indianapolis,* the incident simply would have been considered the result of an enemy action. However, the uproar was too great to conveniently sweep the event under the rug.

The Court of Inquiry is defined in the U.S. Navy Judge Advocate General Manual (JAGMAN) and Judge Advocate General Instructions (JAGINST):

0211 TYPE THREE:
COURTS AND BOARDS OF INQUIRY

a. <u>Overview</u>. Courts and boards of inquiry use a hearing procedure and should be reserved for the investigation of major incidents (as that term is defined in Appendix A-2-a) or serious or significant events. Additional information on the characteristics and conduct of courts and boards of inquiry is set forth in JAGINST 5830.1 series. If there is a conflict with that instruction, this Manual controls.

b. <u>Court of inquiry characteristics</u>
    (1) Convened by persons authorized to convene general courts-martial or so designated by the Secretary of the Navy. (<u>See</u> article 135, UCMJ [*Uniform Code of Military Justice*].)

(2) Consists of at least three commissioned officers as members and also has appointed legal counsel for the court. It may also include advisors appointed to assist the members. (See subsection d below for additional information on advisors.)

(3) Convened by written appointing order.

(4) Uses a hearing procedure. Takes all testimony under oath and records all open proceedings verbatim, except arguments of counsel, whether or not directed to do so in the appointing order.

(5) Designates as parties persons subject to the UCMJ whose conduct is subject to inquiry (see Appendix A-2-b.).

(6) Designates as parties persons subject to the UCMJ or employed by the Department of Defense who have a direct interest in the subject under inquiry and request to be so designated.

(7) Has the power to order military personnel to appear, testify, and produce evidence, and the power to subpoena civilian witnesses to appear, testify, and produce evidence. (Article 47, UCMJ, provides for prosecution of civilian witnesses in U.S. district court for failing to appear, testify, or produce evidence.)

c. Board of inquiry characteristics
    (1) Convened by persons authorized to convene general courts-martial.

(2) Consists of one or more commissioned officers, and should have appointed legal counsel for the board. It may also include advisors appointed to assist the members. (See subsection d below for additional information on advisors.)

(3) Convened by written appointing order, which should direct that all testimony be taken under oath and all open proceedings, except counsel's argument, recorded verbatim. Persons whose conduct is subject to inquiry or who have a direct interest in the subject of the inquiry may be designated parties by the convening authority in the appointing order. The CA [*Convening Authority*] may also authorize the board to designate parties during the proceedings (see Appendix A-2-b).

(4) Uses a hearing.

(5) Does not possess power to subpoena civilian witnesses unless convened under article 135, UCMJ, and Chapter IV, but can order naval personnel to appear, testify, and produce evidence.

d. Advisors. The convening authority may appoint to a court of board of inquiry full-time Federal personnel (military or civilian) to participate in the proceedings and advise the members. Such advisors may be selected because of their subject-matter expertise or because of their background, training, or experience. Advisors may be present at all board or court sessions, are subject to challenge to the same extent as members, and may suggest courses of inquiry or recommend such other action to the board or court as they consider appropriate. Moreover, persons with technical knowledge may be appointed for either full participation or the limited purpose of utilizing their special expertise. If appointed for a limited purpose, they need not participate in any aspect of the inquiry not concerning their expertise. The investigative report must clarify any limited participation by advisors.

e. Responsibilities
(1) The officer exercising general court-martial convening authority over the command most involved in a major or serious incident, if a flag or general officer, or the first

flag or general officer in the chain-of-command, or any superior flag officer in the chain-of-command, will immediately take cognizance over the case as the convening authority.

(2) Whenever more than one command is involved in a major or serious incident requiring formal investigation, a single investigation shall be conducted. The common superior commander shall convene the investigation in such cases, unless that officer's conduct or performance of duty may be subject to inquiry, in which case the next superior in the chain-of-command shall convene the investigation.

f. Convening order. See JAGINST 5830.1 series for the requirements for convening orders for courts and boards of inquiry.

g. Method. See JAGINST 5830.1 series for information on how courts and boards of inquiry are conducted.

h. Participation by non-parties. Other than the official members, counsel, advisors, and administrative support personnel, only parties may, as a general rule, participate in the proceedings of a court or board of inquiry. The CA, or the president in the case of a court of inquiry, may, however, permit the participation of an individual or organization that has an interest in the subject under inquiry. For example, the Federal Aviation Administration may be permitted to participate in an investigation inquiring into the circumstances surrounding an aircraft crash. Appropriate limits on the degree to which such participation may be conditioned should be specified in advance.

i. Time limitations. The CA shall prescribe when the report is due according to the complexity and gravity of the incident under investigation. The CA may grant extensions in writing. Requests and authorizations for extensions must be included in the report as enclosures.

j. Action

(1) Upon receiving a report from a court or board of inquiry, the CA shall review it or cause it to be reviewed, and either endorse the report in writing or return it for further investigation. In the endorsement, the CA may approve, disapprove, modify, or add to the findings of fact, opinions, and recommendations. The CA shall also indicate what corrective action, if any, is warranted and has been or will be taken. The CA shall state in the endorsement where the original evidence is preserved and provide the name and telephone number of the responsible official (see section 0215 for further information on the safekeeping of evidence).

(2) The CA, if not an Echelon II Commander, shall retain a copy of the report and forward the original, via all superior commanders who have a direct official interest in the recorded facts, to the appropriate Echelon II Commander. The subject matter and facts found will dictate the routing of the report for review. Area coordinators or designated subordinate commanders have a direct official interest in incidents that affect their command responsibility or occur in their geographic area. Reports involving Marine Corps matters shall be forwarded to the Commandant of the Marine Corps. The CA shall provide a copy to other commands which may have an interest in the report, such as the Naval Safety Center. (See section 0219 for additional information on routing copies.)

(3) If a court or board of inquiry is to be used as a pretrial investigation under article 32c, UCMJ, and the original report of investigation is desired in connection with trial by general court-martial, it may be retained for such purpose. A complete certified copy shall be forwarded to the Echelon II Commander via appropriate authorities.

(4) The CA's action on the report should be completed within 30 days of receiving the report.

k. <u>Review</u>. Superiors who receive a report from a court or board of inquiry shall have it reviewed, and shall forward it to the cognizant Echelon II Commander, via the chain-of-command. In their endorsements, intermediate reviewing authorities shall comment on the report and stated their concurrence or disagreement with the findings of fact, opinions, and recommendations. They shall also state what action is considered warranted or has been taken. Reports, as a general rule, should be forwarded within 30 days of receipt.

l. <u>Advance copies of investigations</u>.

(1) In all cases where it is appropriate to forward an advance copy of an investigation, the advance copy shall be forwarded by the CA and shall include that officer's endorsement.

(2) All advance copies of Marine Corps investigations shall be forwarded to the Commandant of the Marine Corps after endorsement by the convening authority.

Introduction

*T*HE UNITED STATES Navy has a proud and ex-
tensive tradition of "Don't give up the ship!" The
Navy has cautioned that a Commander "fights to the
last, never strikes the colors, and goes down with the ship,
which never surrendered!" Yet the annals of the U.S. Navy are
replete with examples of those who apparently *did give up the
ship*.

Some Commanders simply let their ship get too close to the
rocks or to shallow water, others failed to zig and zag when
orders were to do so; others were judged to have put their ship in
jeopardy; and still others *simply failed to follow orders*.

Navy Commanders are far different from Army Commanders. The latter can lose themselves and their units, engage in firefights, extricate the Command, and suffer innumerable casualties and not only retain their Command, but are praised for their actions. Army General Anthony McAulife, in December 1944 at Bastogne, lost contact with Headquarters under enemy pressure, yet his action was deemed heroic.

In contrast, the U.S. Navy Commander who strays is excoriated. To be the Commander of a lost cruiser or destroyer is to become a sacrificial lamb in a Court of Inquiry. A different standard prevails.

Perhaps this is due to the possibilities of success. The ship Commander is always operating on the brink of disaster from geology/hydrology — rocks, shoals, wind, weather, seas, or the unexpected (or expected) enemy. The ground Commander is far less circumscribed — he knows where he is, within a general position, and the expected weather. He is confronted with an enemy and he knows the objective. His choices are relatively simple — to take or protect what he has been ordered to do, or to dare and exploit opportunity, but to save as much of his Command as is possible. The U.S. Army says, "Men may come and men may go, but the regiment lives on."

The military Commander has rarely been censored for exploiting an opportunity if he is successful. Leave the order of battle, charge off on your own, and if you succeed you will win praise; if not and the Command is captured or decimated you *may* (repeat *may*) still win praise.

The U.S. Navy counterpart, however, is expected to act in cohesion and ordered cadence; to deviate is insubordinate, even though a measure of success is achieved. Cohesion and mass portend success. The Navy operates within the environment of a "tight ship." Being more hidebound than the U.S. Army, the Navy seldom has given the command of a ship to one who was not of the U.S. Naval Academy tradition. Not many swabs like Admiral Sir John "Jacky" Fisher, of His Majesty's Royal Navy, ever rose to the pilot house. The U.S. Army — except under General George S. Patton — tends to be more casual.

Yet, the expectations of accomplishment of both services are the same.

The U.S. Navy's "mistakes" are seldom publicly known, for they are generally buried in U.S. Navy archives. The recent case of Commander Scott Waddle of the submarine USS *Greenville*, in February 2001, is one of few contemporary exceptions. Most often the Navy, when relieving a ship Commander, simply quietly transferred that officer to shore duty, where a Court of Inquiry met to determine his fate. On the other hand, it has been easy to learn of the career and of the dismissal of an American Infantry Division Commander, for this has been reported to the press..

The classic historical "exception" to Navy policy, of course, occurred after the Pearl Harbor disaster, when Rear Admiral Husband E. Kimmel and U.S. Army Major General Walter C. Short were relieved of duty and excoriated publicly. Thereafter, although the relief of Army Commanders made the press and became the subject of accusations and recriminations, for the most part, the Navy continued — with only a few exceptions forced by the public media — to remain tightlipped, never revealing the circumstances under which a Commander, Captain, or Admiral had lost his Command. If a ship had been sunk by natural causes (rocks), or by enemy action, and inasmuch as the ship no longer existed, a quiet court could either punish or exonerate the former Commander. If the ship was not sunk but simply damaged or put in jeopardy, a quiet transfer could be effected. The World War II case of Captain F. L. Riefkohl of the USS *Indianapolis* was well covered in public accounts and that officer, having lost his ship, was censured (relieved) for failing to have zigged and zagged while in water where enemy submarines were operating.

For an infantry/engineer officer during World War II, the policies of the U.S. Navy are "unbelievable" — ships required to execute close-order drill, yet with vessels of different characteristics in ever-changing sea conditions, all to parade ground precision. If there is indecision, resulting in laggardly response, or if ships collide, the misdemeanor results in "letters in one's file" and doors are closed to future promotions. In contrast, in the U.S. Army the person in responsibility is simply "chewed out" and that is the end of it.

In the main, the consequences of error are so disparate between the U.S. Army and the U.S. Navy that comparison is almost unthinkable. The Army would never put up with officers who simply signed off on inspections that they had never witnessed, and would never tolerate officers not checking on the bearings taken by subordinates, particularly if the certainty of these bearings spelled the very safety of the unit (ship).

To the outside observer, it would appear as if authority has been given to some incapable of exercising it. For two U.S. Army units to engage each other in mortal combat, each not knowing that the other was friendly, would be almost *unthinkable*. Yet for two Navy ships to bear down on each other in the open sea happens all too frequently. Such is not a result of the *variance of improbability* — more likely, it is the result of "neglecting the possible."

The four tragic U.S. Navy incidents that follow all had their quotient of public curiosity and righteous indignation, which caused the U.S. Navy to hold a Court of Inquiry.

Chapter One

"The Gulf Will Wash Us Down" — The USS *Bache*

Death closes all; but something ere the end,

Some work of noble note may yet be done,

Not unbecoming men that strove with Gods.

The lights begin to twinkle from the rocks;

The long day wanes; the slow moon climbs; the deep

Moans round with many voices.

— "Ulysses," Alfred Lord Tennyson

HE USS *Bache* lay quietly at anchor in the harbor of Rhodes, in the Greek Dodecanese Islands, on the night of February 7, 1968. Little did she know, with her furnace cold and her steam gone, that in a few short moments she would soon die, ingloriously, upon the nearby rocks.

The *Bache* was a Fletcher Class destroyer, laid down in 1942 and completed in 1943 at the Brooklyn Navy Yard, one of 119 of this class that had been completed during the years 1942-1945. It has been said that this was the most successful ship class in the long history of the U.S. Navy.

Like all her sisters, the *Bache* had a standard displacement of 2,100 tons (3,050 tons at full load), with a length of 376½ feet, beam of 39½ feet, and draft of 18 feet. With two geared turbines, totaling 60,000 shp (shaft horsepower), she could easily come up to her maximum speed of 35 knots. Fourteen officers and 239 sailors made up her crew. Her senior officer, a Commander or a Lieutenant Commander, always had been an Annapolis graduate, except when she was sitting on the rocks in Rhodes harbor in 1968.

The *Bache* carried five 5-inch guns, two forward and three aft; six 3-inch antiaircraft guns; ten 21-inch torpedo tubes; and two fixed hedge-hogs (antisubmarine mortars), which fired multiple depth bombs.

At the Brooklyn Navy Yard the *Bache* was painted "Pacific Blue," confirming her wartime destination. On leaving the slip, she backed into the submarine net. She cruised in the open sea to Norfolk, Virginia, where she lay for several days, after which she joined the British carrier HMS *Victorious* and two sister destroyers, the USS *Converse* and *Pringle*. Together they sailed to Panama where they traversed the locks to the Pacific Ocean. On the voyage to Pearl Harbor, those on the *Bache* witnessed several crashes while planes attempted to land on the *Victorious*. The battleship USS *Maryland* and six destroyers had also joined the convoy sometime after the *Bache* had cleared the Panama Canal.

While at Pearl, the *Bache* had seen the damage to the fleet that had occurred on December 7, 1941. She had seen the USS *Oklahoma* after it had been pumped out, riding on an even keel, flying her colors. Out in the

Pacific she made a speed run and did 35 knots, though her crew thought she could do better if pressed.

On May 10, 1943, the *Bache* left Pearl Harbor to join the flattop USS *Enterprise*, the battleship *Mississippi*, and the cruiser *New Orleans*, heading for the Aleutian Islands, where the Japanese had landed, without being discovered for some time, challenging American sovereignty. The proud ships were to join others who would have a stiff fight to defeat the invaders and retake the islands.

The USS *Bache* arrived in the Aleutian Islands, westward of Alaska, on May 17th, 1943, and after refueling, picked up a troop transport and made her way to Attu, the westernmost of the Aleutians, where she began shelling Japanese shore positions. On May 21st, she quit Attu and made to sea to join the cruisers *Salt Lake City* and *Pensacola* on their way for Adak. The ships had a rendezvous with the Japanese Admiral Hosagaya who had sent two cruisers, the *Maya* and *Nachi*, to escort two fast merchantmen to re-supply the Japanese garrison on Attu. The cruiser USS *Richmond,* already on picket duty, had been warned of the imminent arrival of a Japanese re-supply force.

The two forces met as the Japanese were approaching Attu. The American cruisers opened fire, and soon the *Salt Lake City* had scored several hits on the *Nachi*. Sensing that the merchant ships were in mortal danger, Hosagawa decoyed the American cruisers away from their quarry.

The *Salt Lake City*, an old ship, was firing vigorously at odd and unnatural angles at the Japanese cruisers and the merchantmen. Thus she severely damaged her steering mechanism and subsequently was able to turn only with great difficulty. The *Bache* and other screening destroyers laid smoke in which the *Salt Lake City* could hide, but the Japanese found her and scored a serious but not incapacitating hit. The Task Force Commander, Rear Admiral Charles H. McMorris, realized that in her damaged condition and with the Japanese scoring hits, the *Salt Lake City* was doomed unless something could be done.

History books refer to the engagement as the "Battle of the Pips" or the "Battle of the Fog Banks." Picture two dueling naval forces steaming into a meeting to take place port to port. Smoke hid the Americans, but the Japanese loosed a bombardment on the sensed location of the *Salt Lake*

City, inflicting so much damage that she was virtually "dead in the water." Admiral McMorris ordered his port-side destroyers to come to their full speed (32 knots — to match the maximum speed of the slowest in the group). This done, he commanded them to make a hard port (left) turn for a desperate torpedo run on the Japanese force.

The USS *Bache* historian, Chief Petty Officer Frisbee, wrote:

> We, the destroyers, went to flank speed, 32 knots, made a hard left turn and started on a torpedo run, always a last ditch maneuver, as a destroyer's life is calculated in minutes, something like 1½ after they are discovered. We steamed at high speed for about 15 to 29 minutes and then secured from GQ [*General Quarters*] as our targets had either disappeared or were non-existent.

What CPO Frisbee did not know was that Japanese Admiral Hosagaya had become alarmed by the audacious torpedo run of the Americans. He surmised that it was either a desperate suicide move or a show of strength, and that the U.S. Navy was about to follow the destroyers with something even more formidable, trapping his ships and sinking them. Whatever Hosagaya's reason, he turned his forces hard aport and broke off the engagement. McMorris wisely did not follow, for he had achieved what he wished — he had denied the re-supply of the garrison. Thanks to the torpedo run of the destroyers, the naval battle of the Aleutians had ended.

The USS *Bache* lay around several Aleutian harbors until August 15th when she began shelling the harbor at Kiska, the 20-mile-long island near the western end of the Aleutian chain. On the 17th, she witnessed the destroyer USS *Abner Reed* strike a mine and become disabled. In late September, the *Bache* was ordered to San Francisco, but her visit was cut short for she was immediately ordered to return to the Aleutians. She spent October and until mid-November on patrol. On November 19th she joined ships bound for Komandorskie Islands, in the Bering Sea, in search of Japanese shipping. She returned to Pearl Harbor on December 4th.

The *Bache* remained at Pearl Harbor for several days and then joined a Task Force, which included two other destroyers, the USS *Ammen* and the

USS *Bush*. They steamed to New Guinea, where they arrived on December 21st. On Christmas Day, *Bache* headed for Cape Gloucester, Queensland, Australia, in the company of the USS *Phoenix* and *Nashville*, two Australian cruisers, the U.S. destroyers *Bush* and *Mullaney,* and two Australian destroyers, the *Arunta* and the *Warramunga*. Anchored off the Cape, they waited all day amidst incessant Japanese air attacks. In the late afternoon they quit their anchorage and began convoying LSTs (Landing Ship, Tank) back to Buna, on the northern shores of New Guinea. They passed the oil slick in the water, marking the place where the destroyer *Bronson* had been sunk only hours before by a Japanese submarine.

On January 3rd, 1944, the convoy arrived in Buna. On the evening of the 5th, they escorted a convoy of LSTs to Cape Gloucester. Upon arrival, January 7th, the ships immediately turned around and began the return to Buna. They rested at their destination for a few days and then set off to return, but en route they were diverted to Finschafen, Papua New Guinea. For the next month they shuttled between Buna, Cape Gloucester, and Finschafen, after which, on February 5th, they were underway for Australia for rest and ship refitting.

After some fun in Sydney and on the beach at Manly, the crew of the *Bache* assembled and sailed back to New Guinea, where the ship was joined by three cruisers and three destroyers, and then steamed on to the Admiralty Islands, part of the Bismarck Archipelago in the southwest Pacific. Upon arrival, the *Bache* shelled and helped silence the Japanese shore batteries that had sunk the U.S. destroyer *Mullaney*.

Thereafter, the USS *Bache* was engaged in support of the island-hopping campaign, which General Douglas MacArthur was waging to reclaim the territory that Japan had taken in the relentless sweep through the islands to the south in the winter of 1941 and 1942. The *Bache*'s "War Action Report" describes one such incident that took place in 1944:

> At 1828 several enemy planes were sighted to starboard. One Tony [*Kawasaki Ki-61*] was destroyed by main battery. The other two enemy planes began a glide suicide approach at this time and one, a Tony, breaking up as a result of 40mm hits, overshot as he crossed from starboard to port, inflicting slight

The USS *Bache* aground in Rhodes Harbor.

damage to the forecastle and crashed into the sea without exploding. The other crashed aboard the USS MACOMB and a large fire blazed for a short time before it was brought under control.

In the course of her adventures, the unfortunate *Bache* was at Okinawa on May 13, 1945, when two kamikaze suicide aircraft attacked her *at the same time*. Upon sighting, the two planes were shot out of the sky. While the antiaircraft guns were busy with the first two, a third kamikaze came from nowhere and crashed amidship. The explosion severely damaged the destroyer; however, she was able to continue the fight until it became apparent that she was of no further use to the invasion. The USS *Bache* had suffered 32 wounded and 41 dead or missing. She returned to Pearl Harbor for repairs, after which she continued on picket — early warning, or lookout — duty in the Pacific until the end of the war, August 15, 1945.

For two years, until January 1947, the USS *Bache* remained on active duty, but then she was decommissioned on the East Coast. The Korean War (1950-1953) brought her out of mothballs, and after undergoing modifications at the Boston Naval Shipyard, she returned to sea as a submarine killer. Though she tried valiantly, there were but few enemy submarines and she recorded no kills.

After Korea, the *Bache* remained active, cruising the Mediterranean Sea to the Middle East, to Europe, and the Caribbean. The destroyer was an active participant in the Cuban Blockade in 1962 and then in the later Haitian crisis. She took a patrol station off Cyprus during a crisis there, and in 1964 off Zanzibar. During the 1965 unrest in the Dominican Republic, the destroyer was anchored in Guantánamo Bay, Cuba.

The next four years of her life were spent doing what she did best — sailing the oceans of the world — a proud and resolute ship that wore her ribbons well. In 1967, the USS *Bache* began once again the Mediterranean and Aegean Seas cruise that took her, on February 5, 1968, to the harbor of Rhodes, and death.

Overhead aerial view of the USS *Bache* aground in Rhodes Harbor.

Edward A. Broadwell, who had been Commander of the USS *Bache* for 15 months, describes the arrival in Rhodes and the selection of an anchorage:

Commander Edward A. Broadwell, of the USS *Bache,* grounded at Rhodes.

> On the morning of February 5, we arrived in Rhodes on what is described as an Operational Visit (low key). We had anticipated that we would be given a berth (which might require abandonment if the wind came up) but we were directed to an anchorage area and we picked our own location as being clear of the fairway and in about 17 fathoms (a fathom is 6 feet) of water. I got the chain out and after a heavy pull at first it slacked off to a light lull. The wind was from the east (southeast) at 15-18 knots. I anchored inside the 25-fathom mark because with the amount of chain that a destroyer normally carries this is a desirable maximum depth so that the scope (length) of chain versus depth of water should provide the textbook requirements of 5 or 7 to 1. The pilot boat did come out and after a little difficulty understanding his signals we came to the location which he and I agreed upon.

Rhodes, where the USS *Bache* met her rendezvous with fate, lies in the Aegean Sea 300 miles southeast of Piraeus, the seaport for Athens. The island, 45 miles long and 20 miles wide, lies in the northeast-southwest direction and is a part of the Dodecanese. The principal terrestrial features are mountains, ranging to 4,000 feet; the greatest in height is named

Attavyros. The mountains are composed of fine-grained marine sediments that are hard and not affected by tectonic activity. At the foot of the prominences lie coastal plains comprised of earth viable for agriculture: weathered limestone and sandstone.

Rhodes has been inhabited since the Bronze Age, and because of its location and size has played a prominent part in the history of the area. The famous 120-foot statue of Apollo, called the Colossus of Rhodes, one of the seven wonders of the ancient world, stood magnificent at the entrance to the Mandraki Harbor. It did not, as is believed, stand with legs spread for ships to sail between them. One of two stone columns, topped by a bronze statue of a deer, stands in the same place today — marking the entrance to the small-craft harbor. A bit farther south is the mercantile or commercial harbor, offering more depth but little berthing, so that ships must anchor in the roadstead. Anchorage is considered good — there is plenty of room to swing on a mooring, and the sea floor is comprised of accumulated marine sediment that is sufficiently dense to hold the pivoted flukes of the anchors.

The weather has been described as idyllic — seldom above 90 degrees F and seldom below 60 degrees F. The wind is reputed to blow incessantly from the west during the months of September through May. In the summer, when the wind is not blowing from the Turkish mainland (from the east), the northeasterly winds moderate the heat. The anomaly is the maverick sirocco wind that blows from the south-southeast often with such violence that ships are advised to remain at sea rather than anchor in the roadstead. Those in the roadstead are then advised to seek shelter in the lee of the island. Small craft moored in the commercial port are safe from the sirocco, but larger craft throughout the ages have been warned of the errant wind.

Because of the protocol of following the advice of one's host, it is generally accepted that a visitor to a port will anchor where told to do so, and with a knowledge of the winds will set sufficient anchor chain to do no harm to another ship anchored nearby but of sufficient length to give holding power (no dragging) for whatever wind or sea should come along. Furthermore, to set two anchors when everyone else has set but one would brand one as a "sissy"; hence when the *Bache* came to the harbor of Rhodes she anchored where told to, set sufficient chain so as to allow swing but not interference with another ship, and pretended to act as any other naval vessel should — proud but not boorish.

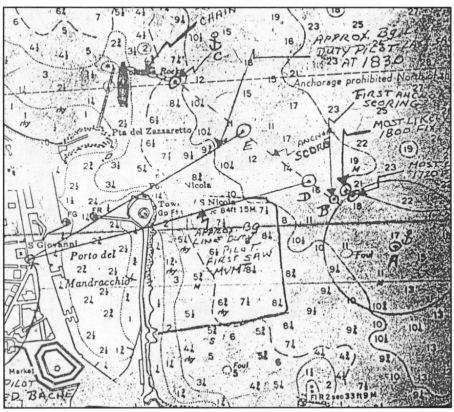

Chart of the track of the USS *Bache* from her anchorage in Rhodes Harbor to her grounding.

In the Court of Inquiry, beginning February 7, 1968, Commander Broadwell testified,

> After anchoring we received the delegation from the shore; Mr.
> [*James B.*] Barker, Voice of America, a Greek man who works
> for Mr. Barker and the Port Captain. They told me that there
> was a Sirocco (a warm moist sea wind which blows on the north
> Mediterranean Coast) and this was too bad because they had
> certain things planned for our visit. After they left the ship I
> went ashore and paid official visits on the Bishop, the Prefect,

the Mayor and the Governor of the Area. I thought that the weather was a little too hazardous to allow these persons to pay a return call, and I told them so. However, I did allow liberty that evening and we had no problems until the last liberty returning at about 2:30 or 3:00 a.m. when the sea started to pick up. At about three a.m. on the morning of the 6th, Lieutenant Weinberger, the duty officer, came and woke me up with a late weather report of a low center to the northwest (west?) of us headed northeast with predicted winds of 35 to 40 knots. He requested permission to veer (*let out*) the (port) anchor to 100 fathoms (I had anchored in at 75 fathoms). I gave permission to do so. He also requested that I allow him to put the engines on stand-by but as we were short of water I only allowed him to put one shaft on line and he elected to put the port shaft on line.

At about eight on the morning the 6th, I directed that the shaft that had been put on stand-by be put on a five minute alert. During the afternoon I spent most of the time on the bridge. I directed the navigator and the leading quartermaster, Mr. Weinberger, who was also the OD [*Officer of the Deck*] and Crumlish, leading quartermaster, to take bearings every ten minutes. I also pointed out to them a natural range that we had (roughly that of lining up two objects which can be seen clearly ashore) and keeping this always in observation and so long as the two objects remain in line, you have your line of position. I also visited the forecastle and checked the anchor chain. It was riding moderately. There was a set that tended to keep the ship from going through full swing at anchor, which it normally does. Usually it will sail up to one end of the anchor, as the wind takes it, gets it on the other bow, it will sail to the other side, and back and forth in that nature. After dinner, at about 1800, I went back to my cabin and shortly after that I noticed that the ship had a different feel. There was no appreciable jerk; maybe it was just the roll of the ship that was different.

There I met the fantail sentry who said that the anchor lights were getting very close or lights on the beach were getting very close. I ran to the bridge and to the pilot house and called main control and told them to get steam on the port engine and rang up port-ahead two-thirds and had people on the forecastle ready to drop the starboard anchor but by that time it was too late. The engine did not get the bell and the shaft wouldn't turn and about this time the rudder was jammed — I believe full left. I got word that the starboard engine was ready to turn and I tried to go ahead with the starboard engine, perhaps getting off. I asked for a heading at this time and it was 000. I got up to 75 turns on the starboard engine and then got word that the after-engine room was flooding and they would have to secure it. The last thing that we lost was the generator. I directed as soon as the chief engineer reported that he could not maintain the position anymore, to wrap up the boilers to prevent a boiler explosion. Finally we went plant dead. The wind and the sea caught us and swung us towards the beach.

The wind was from the southeast about 140 all day and we were swinging to 090 and holding there. After it became apparent that we could do nothing and the ship was undergoing a series of violent crashes, I sent out one message that we were breaking up, and we were. I tried to discharge some oil on the starboard side to calm the sea but this didn't do any good and got thrown all over the ship. I told the engineer to ballast down, hoping that we could settle in rather than bounce in any further. Mr. Barker says we hit stern first but I am sure it was on the port side.

I wasn't sure what would happen to the ship, I didn't know if it would roll over or break apart or just what. I gave the word to prepare to abandon ship and about ten minutes later I gave word to abandon ship. We found a break in the dike, there is a mole [*a breakwater or jetty*] coming out and some stones on the other side of that. There is a light out there and perhaps we could rig a trolley line or a highline between these two points. We did not have a line-throwing gun and there is no way to get a line to us from the beach. We requested tugs and assistance and we were told that there were no tugs in the area. There was no assistance except what we could provide ourselves. I don't know exactly when the first life rafts went overboard. The method was to bring the raft, inflate it and the people jumped. We were close enough to the water on the port side. We positioned the rafts so that they could make it through the break between the small breakwater there and the stones. The first raft we sent light, loaded with 15 or 20 and then we saw how things went and we started loading more on the rafts. There was a strong northerly set, so while still in the lee of the ship, they would drift up northward toward the rocks, and then the wind and seas, sea action took over and they worked their way onto the beach.

Well we continued to put the people ashore in the boats and my plan was to leave myself, the registered pubs custodian, Mr. Sanburn, the navigator, Mr. Weinberger, who is also the top secret officer and a signalman, four of us that were going to spend the night on the ship. This is so the ship wouldn't be abandoned and we wanted to get some of these publications squared away but to get everyone else off the ship. (But as the wind moderated and there appeared to be no danger) we decided to keep everyone (those who remained aboard) aboard and we sent a report to the beach guard officer and to the senior Shore Patrol Officer, and (we remained on board until morning) when the first ships came in and we gave them a status report, and salvage operations commenced. Admiral Kidd, Commodore Davis and Captain Arthur and the rest of the people came aboard and assessed the situation.

Thus was told the story of the beaching of the destroyer USS *Bache* by its Captain, Commander Broadwell. During the Court of Inquiry, more was to be learned from members of the crew who told their own recollections of what had been important in the events preceding as well as on the night of the sinking.

Chief Boatswain's Mate Arthur Erb, Jr., who was in charge of deck details at the time of the grounding, stated that normally when a ship is dragging anchor the chain will slacken and slap the deck of the ship when it becomes taut. In the case of the *Bache* in Rhodes Harbor, he saw no such occurrence, but it seemed that as dragging took place the wind was taking the ship in a steady flow, with no bouncing up or down. It seemed to him that when he was in the Chief's quarters eating the evening meal, about five minutes had elapsed between finishing dinner and the big THUMP that signaled the *Bache* had struck.

In answer to a question by President of the Court of Inquiry Admiral Isaac C. Kidd, Jr., Erb remembered that the destroyer had been anchored in 17 fathoms [*102 feet*] of water. He testified that both of the anchors aboard were of the same weight — 4,000 pounds. The normal length of anchor chain let out is five to seven times the depth of the water. There is, at all times when in port, a port watch whose duty is to provide surveillance of the ship and its environment, as well as its position and to report any changes to the bridge. There had been no snapping of the anchor chain, but Erb knew that the ship was dragging. When the first "bump" came, he had made for the starboard anchor and had already knocked out the stopper pin when Lieutenant Pearson came up hollering, "Drop the anchor!"

When asked if he had left the Chief's quarters for the deck after he had felt the first thump, Erb said that he had, and he had remarked, "It seems like we hit a rock or something."

Erb continued,

> My instructions to all my men was, "If the anchor (chain) is dragging they will be slapping the deck. When an anchor breaks loose it will dig in again, you will have a slack on the chain. When the ship yaws in the chain you will make it just like a hammerhead."
>
> I say, when it does that that is a good indication for suspecting dragging. I will hear it anyway but still I said to get a hold of me and let the bridge know.

James B. Barker, head of the Voice of America in Rhodes, testified about the day of arrival of the destroyer and of the grounding.

> When the *Bache* arrived on Monday morning, February 5th, I arranged to come aboard with the Port Captain and with my senior local — the purpose of the visit was to meet the Captain of the ship and sit down with him and discuss the program for the vessel's visit. Captain [*Demetrias*] Katevenis, the port

Captain, remarked on the weather — we had a rough trip out —
a little difficult for me in getting aboard, and it was a swell —
I think Captain Katevenis and my senior local said it was the
beginning of a sirocco. We then proceeded to discuss the weather under any circumstances (the effect that the weather would
have on the planned program for the ship and crew). We had
also planned to have a luncheon for the official Greek community, Tuesday, February 6th. However, by Tuesday morning the
sea had built up and I think the wind was stronger to the point
where Captain Broadwell I understand felt that we could not get
people out there safely, so the luncheon was canceled. — As
late as 5 p.m. I spoke to Lieutenant McCracken and asked him
if there was still any possibility of the ship's officer compliment
coming ashore. He said that he did not believe so, that the seas
and the wind were still quite high. — At five minutes after
seven I got a call from the Port Authority advising me that the
Bache appeared to be going on the reef at the entrance to the
harbor, so I got down there within five minutes and I would say
that the ship was virtually on the reef, she appeared to have
come in stern first and then broached in the wind and was I
think pretty much on the reef when I first saw it. — The *Bache*
was receiving them (breakers) on her starboard side, sprays
perhaps 60 to 70 feet high, I would judge.

In further testimony Barker estimated that the wind velocity on the
point, where the *Bache* had been anchored, to have been close to 50 knots.
He stated that the anchorage where the destroyer lay was the established
one for visiting ships of any kind and that it was there that the cruise ships
anchored. The Port Authority or the Port Captain had assigned the anchorage area to the *Bache*. In a sirocco, with wind from the south or southeast,
the harbor is closed to all traffic. He stated that it was the practice for ships
caught on this side to go to the lee side of the island. He said that he had
come to understand that siroccos, which develop in Africa, pick up considerable velocity as they cross the Mediterranean.

Lieutenant Weinberger, the navigator of the *Bache* testified:

I picked a position (for anchoring) that was apparently well sheltered as could be within the harbor and not too deep. I picked a point that had 16 to 17 fathoms of water and we dropped the hook within 30 yards of the point I picked. — As I remembered reading the night before in the sailing directions there was good holding ground in the area. Rather than let out a long chain, we let out 75 fathoms of chain so we would have more room to swing in case the wind came out as the nearest shoal water was to the south of us. It was very calm.

I stood the 4 to 8 watch on the morning of the 6th, and the wind had picked up appreciably, the seas were kicking up and about, I believe it was about 4:30 or 5 in the morning, I advised the Captain that I was going to veer chain to 100 fathoms and we were going to make the starboard anchor ready to let go. About 1500, I moved the quarterdeck watch to the bridge to supervise the bearing-taking watch and the position of the ship. At about 1800, I went up to the bridge and looked around and saw the 1800 fix. It was the position we had been in throughout the day. The Quartermaster was taking a couple of sights then. I listened to him call off the sight. The bearings were the same that I remembered for all day for the two points I heard him call. The anemometer was out – it had been out for as long as I can remember. I went down to radio central, which is one ladder down, to check and see if the last weather message would indicate what the storm was doing. I found no messages on the board — I was down there maybe ten minutes or so. I felt a bump. We bumped again and — took off for the bridge. As I arrived on the bridge I looked out towards the anchor — the anchor chain was across the stern and back. I ran off to the Port side and saw rocks there. I was pretty sure we were aground. — The only place we could get the people off the ship onto the rafts was amidships, port side. There was a large fishing vessel off our starboard side that seemed to be trying to make us. It was totally out of the question. He got within 100 yards. He was putting a light on us. In fact, his light led to some confusion. We attempted to shoot line guns over the breakwater but to no avail. — Previously in the day, when we anchored, I told them (bridge watch) (to take bearings) every twenty minutes. The Captain informed them every ten minutes.

Lieutenant Weinberger was reminded that he remained under oath, and the court, during recess, visited the ship. As the court resumed, Weinberger continued his testimony. He was asked by Admiral Kidd to return to the *Bache* after he finished testifying, and try to find the piece of acetate that had been used to plot positions on the chart in the period before the grounding.

Admiral Kidd asked, "At what time have we best established as her time of first grounding?"

Captain Boston, a member of the Court of Inquiry, replied, "1835 to 1837, but it will come out more definitely later."

Admiral Kidd stated,

> I think the important thing for an individual reading the record to note here is that (Bearing Log) reflects bearing frequency in the neighborhood of 20 minutes apart during the period immediately prior to the grounding. . . . Let the record further show that from the evidence thus far available it appears as though the first movement of the ship towards the beach from her previously relatively static position, allowing for movement incident to normal swinging probably occurred subsequent to the last recorded time in the bearing book log of 1800. The Navigator testified that he had personally sighted the duty Quartermaster taking bearings subsequent to 1800, and prior to the time he, the Navigator went below to the radio shack at about 1820 —.

When asked by Admiral Kidd, Lieutenant Weinberger replied,

> I instructed the Quartermaster that if none of the bearings differed by more than a degree, they did not have to plot it, however, they were to plot often enough that if they just had one round, and then went I didn't want them to go any amount, several hours, without plotting, that they should plot every half hour.

Admiral Kidd asked Weinberger if, after anchoring, the ship had swung through 360 degrees or had it maintained a relatively continuous ship's heading of the southeast direction, to which he replied,

> The ship was never in any quadrant from approximately 250 counterclockwise around to 030 during the time that I observed until I actually came up to the bridge. At that point the ship's head was toward north around 030 or perhaps 000.

Admiral Kidd then stated that the record should show that the anchor chain and the anchor had been inspected by divers and found to be intact.

When asked if he had had any prior experience with a dragging anchor, Weinberger replied,

> In Beaulieu, France, we were anchored just possibly a little closer to the beach than this and I detected the anchor apparently dragging and we got underway and moved further out. — The first noticeable symptom, it happened almost simultaneously. The anchor watch thought it was dragging and the bearing takers noticed it.

Ensign Charles T. Wilson, Jr., Damage Control Officer, a Reservist who had been in the Navy for nearly two years and on the *Bache* for nearly ten months testified:

> The messenger, after I relieved him said he would have to go down to find the anchor watch because there was no growler [*intra-ship telephone communication*] on that part of the ship and he was going down to get reports every so often. — He said that he had trouble finding him [*the anchor watch*] that he was in the bos'n locker. I sent him back down to tell the anchor watch not to leave the anchor, to stay right there, not to leave the anchor chain. This was probably about 1615 — well I'd say about a half hour later, probably 1645, I made a round. Then I walked up to the forecastle and saw the anchor watch standing in front of Mount 51. I told him not to go down to the bos'n

locker, to stand the watch and not to take his eyes off the anchor chain. — It was 1835, by the clock — the anchor watch called from the fantail, I mean called from the after deck house and said that there were some rocks close by. — I got on the 21MC [*the multi-communication system*] and asked main control how long it would be before they could give me steam and they said they had it on the way up, probably take two or three minutes. — Shortly thereafter it felt like the stern hit the rocks and then we went to general quarters.

Admiral Kidd required that the record show that during the critical period of the two or three hours prior to grounding, the bearing book showed only two plots per hour rather than the three that a frequency of every 20 minutes would require. He then asked, "Now you made a statement that interests me in relation to the anchor watch and it seems that I recall your saying that he called you from some place back aft. Is that correct?"

Wilson answered in the affirmative.

Kidd then asked, "How could he watch the anchor and be back aft?"

Wilson replied, "I – I – He couldn't."

The court then asked Wilson if, when he came back on watch, had he asked, before relieving the watch, "Is everything the same?"

And the court added, "Your indication of the position of ship was exclusively a plot on the chart?"

To each of these Wilson had answered in the affirmative.

Admiral Kidd then made a startling statement. "The court at this point designates this young gentleman as an interested party. Do you understand what that means, son?"

Wilson replied, "Yes Sir."

Kidd continued as he addressed Wilson, "It is for your own protection and it gives you certain additional rights. You can sit here and listen to what everybody else says. It doesn't imply culpability. It doesn't imply negligence. It doesn't imply anything other than a right to you to be very much interested, personally and professionally, as to what is going on."

Captain Padgett then asked Wilson, "Between the hour of, when you returned up to the bridge at 1805, until the grounding, you didn't see any bearings taken?"

Wilson replied, "No Sir."

Wilson acknowledged that he knew what an anchor buoy was and he had not observed whether he had one on his port anchor. Though not sure about the actual characteristics, he was sure that the engine he had available in case of an emergency could be brought to action by merely turning one valve and it would be delivering power in five minutes.

The court asked, "Suppose that you had gotten timely warning by a definite indication from bearing changes that you were dragging, from your training and indoctrination and experience, what would you do?"

Wilson replied, "First I would have notified Mr. Weinberger."

When Wilson had taken the watch, he knew that the steering motors were not on. Also, at that time he had observed the rudder to be left 5 to 10 degrees.

Commander Broadwell then asked, "During the afternoon of the 6th, were you called by Mr. Weinberger and asked to light off the steering engine?"

Wilson replied that he had done so "some time during the day." Wilson then recounted that when Weinberger had told him to light off the steering motor, he had checked with the Chief Engineer and realized it necessary to man the space to light it off when needed, and he told Mr. Weinberger this. At the close of his testimony, Ensign Wilson was asked by Lieutenant Weinberger what had been his reply when Weinberger had asked him if he was sure that he could have the steering motor in a time of two or three minutes? Wilson said he had replied to Weinbeger in the affirmative.

Ensign John F. Dolan, the Anti-Submarine Warfare (ASW) Officer, then testified:

> At about 1805, Mr. Wilson called me down on the growler to get me out of bed. I was suppose to relieve him for chow at about 1800. I got up to the bridge about 1810 and relieved him. There were only two things that happened on the watch, the anchor lights burned out twice. They were repaired. About 1820, Admiral, I don't know what time it was, I wasn't looking at the time, there was a fix taken because I compared the

bearings of the last fix with bearings of the fix before. There was no appreciable difference. The bearings were on the line.

Kidd asked Dolan if the bearings plotted or those compared with were recorded in a book, Dolan stated that they were not recorded in a book but were written on pieces of plain paper lying on the plotting board.

Ensign Dolan said, "At 1810, I got a report that the anchor was tending to 1 o'clock moderate strain from the forecastle watch."

Kidd asked Dolan how many bearings he actually saw taken during the time he was on the bridge, to which Dolan replied, "At least one, Admiral, I don't know if they took more."

The court, along with Commander Broadwell and Lieutenant Weinberger, both interested parties, visited and interviewed Captain Alexander Ionanou, South Aegean Hellenic Naval Forces, and Commander Demetrias Katevenis, Port Captain of Rhodes.

Commander Broadwell, "Was it normal for ships to anchor in that position?"

"Yes."

"Was the man who came out to direct the positioning of the *Bache* at anchor satisfied with the anchoring?"

"Yes."

Captain Lauff, "Was the pilot who observed and directed the ship in anchoring completely satisfied with the position in which the anchor was let go?"

"Yes."

Captain Ionanou, "In that precise area I believe the bottom to be sand although the chart is marked mud. In general, the roadstead is rocky."

Commander Katevenis, Port Captain, "At approximately 1830, I was called by my duty officer who was then in his flat above his office and he notified me that the *Bache* was moving but he did not believe that it was underway and under control. When I questioned him about the speed of movement he said that it was moving fast enough to attract his attention."

Admiral Kidd, "She was dragging anchor somewhere around 1825-1835 and grounded at about 1845. This would mean that she probably traveled approximately 1,000 yards in at least some fifteen minutes, which would give her a speed over ground of 50 to 70 yards per minute. I was told that the anchorage in which the *Bache* initially positioned herself was a long-standing approved in which many ships, in years gone by, have ridden out heavy weather as bad or worse than that experienced during the day and evening of Tuesday, February 6th. When asked about notifying ships in the harbor about bad weather conditions, I was told that it was the positive conviction of local Hellenic authorities that ships of naval classes would have better weather information available to them from radio reports and from installation equipment than from local authorities."

Captain Lauff, "It is for these reasons that the Hellenic Harbor Authorities did not attempt to advise naval vessels of weather conditions."

Boatswain's Mate Fred A. Holloway testified:

In my professional knowledge the best way to determine if an anchor is dragging is to put your foot on it (the taut chain) and if you get a vibration on it (the chain) to see if it (the anchor) is dragging. This is the way I checked it (the anchor chain) and I had no feel of vibration.

Lieutenant Clyde Louis Carter, the Engineering Officer stated:

The morning of 6 February, I contacted CPO Holbrook and asked him what the status of the plant was and was informed that we were on a steaming status, No. 2 Plant on the line. I questioned him concerning the time, the minimum limit in which we could get the plant underway. At that time he stated that under normal conditions we could be underway in fifteen minutes. I reiterated my question to "What is the minimum time you can have the plant on the line?" He said, "Well, Mr. Carter, you give me five minutes, more likely two, and I can have this ship steaming." At approximately 1830-1840, that evening I was sitting in my stateroom with the Main Propulsion Assistant, Lieutenant (JD) Taylor. We felt a thump or grinding bump on the ship. Mr. Taylor asked me, "What was that?" I didn't say anything immediately but the ship made another lurch or bump, and I said, "I believe we are dragging anchor." From the phone on my desk I talked to the engine room. I asked them if they had received any bells or other transmissions from the bridge and their answer was negative. I told them to cross-connect the plant and get all steam available to the plant immediately. I went to the engine room and was told by Machinist's Mate Nunn that he was receiving bells (from the bridge) but the port jacking gear [*for raising the cable*] was frozen. I went to the jacking gear and a man was standing on the release lever, bouncing, trying to free the jacking box. — The Captain ordered me to order all spaces secured and prepare to abandon ship. When we had no more communications (from the bridge) I called the bridge and told them that Chief Holbrook and I were the last personnel in main control, we were evacuating and going off the line.

The court then recessed to hear a statement from a Greek citizen employed as a pilot in the Port Captain's Office. He testified that when he was on watch outside the Port Captain's Office, on the night of February 6th, at about 1830, he had noticed that something was wrong with the position of the ship. He first had seen it to the right side of St. Nicholas Tower, which is located on the breakwater, and then noticed it to the left. He could see it was moving. He indicated that the ship continued to maintain a heading of 045-070 until she hit, and then she had swung into a northerly heading. He did not actually see her hit the sea wall, for he had not returned from his call to the Port Captain before the collision.

The court then was informed that per its instruction, Lieutenant Weinberger had gone to the ship and had returned with a piece of acetate that had covered the plotting board at the time of grounding. For the court he identified the various positions shown on the clear acetate and told what they were and their use during the course of plotting, which occurred immediately before the grounding. Weinberger testified that wind speed and its direction were estimated because the ship's anemometer had been broken for more than a month and the tender in Naples would not repair it.

Quartermaster Crumlish was then asked what his duties were ("taking and recording bearings and plotting the course of the ship") and when he had described these, the president of the court, Admiral Kidd, took him through some exercises to determine the nature of the procedures that were used aboard the USS *Bache* in taking and recording data that denoted the position of the ship.

Ensign John Dolan was recalled as a witness at his own request. He stated that he had come on the bridge from having been stationed on deck in order to observe the anchor chain, and he had reported the condition of tautness of the anchor chain (strain) to the Captain, and at that time had identified, by his own observation, the tower of St. Angelo. He recalled that the Quartermaster he had seen (on the bridge) was Quartermaster Jones — he never saw Crumlish. He recalls that when he came to the bridge at 1810 he had checked the readings that were then being made and compared these with the previous readings and concluded that they were close enough to believe that the ship had not moved and that the minor discrepancies were but human error in reading. Though it was night, he had had no difficulty in identifying the objects ashore, which were being used in position plotting. (Admiral Kidd inserted in the record that the hour about which Ensign Dolan was speaking was 1825 local time and "pitch black dark.") Dolan recounted communications that he had with the anchor watch who reported that the anchor, while not dragging, was under strain. Admiral Kidd painstakingly went over position taking and position plotting with Dolan. Dolan recalled that after he had been relieved, he went below, and while talking with Lieutenant Pearson, he felt three "bumps" in the ship.

Seaman Alfred Jones, Quartermaster Striker, testified that he had returned to the bridge at about 1840 and had looked at the bearing book first.

> At this time Mr. Wilson came in and said that we were moving, so I went out and shot two bearings and as soon as I got these two bearings we hit the rocks. From then we went to general quarters.

It was established, by questioning, that some of the plots of the position of the ship were different from others and this might have led to the conclusion that either the ship had moved or some of the readings had been incorrect. In the testimony it was established that as dark had approached, one of the "on-shore" bearing references had been shifted from the tower of St. Angelo to a light located 70 yards to the west of the tower. It was established that if the new bearing reference (light) had been located as being the old reference (tower), this incorrect assumption could explain discrepancies, if such existed in the positions plotted after day had ended. Jones informed the court that the plotting device that had been used to show the instrumented position of the ship was a "universal drafting machine."

The court then heard from Commander John Boyd and Captain Russell Arthur, both engineering officers who were qualified as experts and who had examined the condition of the *Bache* as related to the extent of damages she had sustained and the possibility of salvaging (repairing) her. Both officers stated that it would be possible to refloat the destroyer but that to refloat her for the purpose of repairs would not be feasible. Commander J. B. MacCaffrey of the U.S. Coast Guard also assisted the damage/repairability survey officers, and his report was also introduced, which concurred with that of the two naval officers.

Firecontrolman Third Class Terry Schmidt testified that he had been Fetty Officer of the bridge watch from 1600 until 2000 and had been there at about 1800. Schmidt said that the anchor watch [*Seaman Apprentice John*] Dighero had called at approximately 6:30 on the growler and wanted to speak to Mr. Wilson. When Wilson came to the phone he (the anchor watch) said something to the effect that "we were drifting and when I looked I saw that we were pretty close to the rocks."

Electronics Technician Radar Seaman (ETRSN) John Mandella, who was messenger of the watch, testified that because the ship's port-side Med-lights — "Mediterranean lights," the string of lights outlining the ship while in a foreign port — were not burning, he had fetched an electrician who repaired them, and then he was instructed to visit the post of the anchor watch and to return with information concerning the condition of the chain and anchor.

> I returned with the information that the anchor was tending to one-o'clock with moderate strain. The med-lights went out again and, as I was on the growler, about to speak with the electrician I heard that we were close to the rocks. After that there were a lot of people on the bridge.

Seaman Apprentice John Dighero, who had been the anchor watch during the period of interest, stated that from the forecastle it was not possible to see much of the position of the ship related to land, so that he had to go amidship to get a good look. From such a position he saw that the stern was getting very close to the rocks: "I informed Mr. Wilson of this and also saw the Captain, standing under the whaleboat and told him the same thing." He then felt something, a dragging motion, which he described (while standing on the stern) as "going round in circles." He notified the bridge by the growler that the anchor was dragging. He said that he had a different feeling, at the time just before the ship struck the rocks, in the way the ship felt beneath his feet.

Admiral Kidd stated that a diver had examined the position and state of the anchor and had reported that the anchor was well imbedded at the time of inspection, but that there was a "straight tend [*direction*] now from hawse pipe [*the reinforced conduit channel through which the anchor chain passes*] to hook," which led Kidd to the conclusion that the anchor had tumbled from the time it had come loose until just before it had stopped. Members of the court and interested parties then discussed with Dighero the sensations of "anchor dragging," his training, his length of service, and whether or not he had ever previously "felt" an anchor, which was *known* to be dragging.

When the testimony of the witnesses had been concluded, the president of the court read from Navy regulations the duties of a ship's Captain and of an Executive Officer. Commander Broadwell then spoke of his prior Navy experience, of the condition of the *Bache*, and the level of training and experience of her crew. He concluded that it was his responsibility for the safety of the ship.

The counsel for the court spoke last and reiterated the doctrine of law "*res ipsa loquitur*," which means "the thing speaks for itself." The Court of Inquiry issued its findings, subject to U.S. Navy review and approval or modification.

After review and the time for appeal having expired, the findings of the court stood.

The USS *Bache*, having lain on the rocks for many months, subject to the prying eyes of those who came to Rhodes, was subsequently committed to the salvage crews who cut her, piece by piece, into scrap.

The "Preliminary Statement" of the court and the "Finding of Fact" follow, along with the "Summary" of the occurrence in which the court had drawn its conclusions. There was no allusion to the fate of Commander Broadwell. However, he did receive a reprimand.

PRELIMINARY STATEMENT

This Court of Inquiry was convened pursuant to the verbal orders of Commander in Chief, U.S. Naval Forces, Europe which were telephonically communicated to the President of the Court at or about 1210 hours, 7 February 1968. The appointed President alerted the counsel and a party of twelve pertinent naval personnel who proceeded via U.S. Navy C-13 aircraft from Naples, Italy, departing at 0400 hours, 7 February 1968, arriving in Rhodes, Greece, 0730 hours, 7 February 1968 and who then proceeded to the stranded USS BACHE (DD 470) [*Destroyer 470*] lying broached to alongside a concrete breakwater contiguous to the beach water front. No unusual problems arose incident to the subject proceedings except for the necessity to conclude the said proceedings in the most expeditious manner possible since timely removal salvage action was imperative to avoid possible oil contamination of a very popular, exclusive local tourist beach and the more cogent consideration was that the naval vessel's ammunition placed the surrounding area in jeopardy by possible detonation. Also, all personnel who had been evacuated from USS BACHE were billeted in local hotels which placed an unusual burden on the local community even though the local populace evinced the highest level of hospitality and consideration.

As reflected by the record of proceedings, the Court met almost continuously night and day until adjournment in Rhodes, Greece. The members and counsel then proceeded to Naples, Italy for deliberation and preparation of the record.

The Court, after inquiring into all the facts and circumstances connected with the incident which occasioned the inquiry, and having considered the evidence, finds as follows and submits the following opinions and recommendations:

FINDING OF FACT

1.   That USS BACHE was visiting Rhodes on a properly cleared and duly authorized operational visit directed by appropriate and competent authority. (R. 2)

2. That the berth in which the USS BACHE anchored was selected by the Commanding Officer after consultation with the navigator and after studying appropriate navigational documents and official Navy Port Information Pamphlets. (R. 2)

3. That the anchorage selected conformed with such official documents. (R. 3)

4. That as the ship approached the selected berth prior to anchoring, a uniformed official in a launch from the harbor signaled to the Commanding Officer with hand signals to move further to the southeast before actually letting go. The aforementioned hand signals from the official harbor launch were complied with by the Commanding Officer, USS BACHE. (R. 3) The aforementioned Greek official's superior was subsequently interviewed by the members of the Court of Inquiry. This Greek official, the Port Director and a Commander in the Hellenic equivalent of the U.S. Coast Guard, stated the berth in which BACHE anchored was safe for her and satisfactory to the Port Authorities. (R. 80)

5. That USS BACHE dropped the port anchor at 0954, 6 February 1968, after approaching the berth on a southeasterly heading, making slight sternway at the time of letting go. (Ex. 10-58) (R. 20)

6. That an anchor buoy was attached to the port anchor but was not watching [*sic*] from the time of anchoring until sometime after the ship stranded. There were approximately 19 fathoms of line attaching the anchor buoy to the port anchor. (R. 24)

7. That 75 fathoms of chain were veered in 11 fathoms of water as recorded in the Quartermaster's

Notebook (chart plot indicated about 15) while setting up the brake periodically as the chain paid out, to insure a good bite on the bottom. (R. 19, 21, 22) (Ex. 10-58 and Ex. 2)

8.   That the available weather reports indicated a low to the northwest of Rhodes which was expected to move northeastward slowly and if this prediction developed, winds in the Rhodes anchorage would have been expected to shift from the southeast, clockwise, toward the southwest which would cause the ship's heading to shift from a southeasterly heading to a safe southwesterly heading and give the ship the benefit of the lee provided by the land mass. (R. 4, 5)

9.   That during the day on Monday the 5th, wind and weather in Rhodes anchorage continued moderate with wind generally from the southeast. (R. 42)

10. That late in the day of Monday the 5th, the wind from the southeast began to increase but not to a dangerous degree. (R. 42)

11. That during the course of the night of the 5th, the wind intensity increased to a point where the Chief Boatswain's Mate, on his return from liberty about midnight, decided to go to the forecastle to examine his ground tackle carefully. (R. 25)

12. That sometime during the 0400 and 0800 watch on the morning of the 6th, the wind had increased to a point where the navigator, Lieutenant (junior grade) Weinberger, was prompted to call the Commanding Officer and recommend to him that the readiness of the engines be increased and the port anchor chain be veered. (R. 4, 42)

13. That the Commanding Officer received the afore-
    mentioned recommendation and decided only to veer
    chain for the following judgment reasons: (R. 4)

    a. The fact that the ship only had 50% feed
       water on board dictated to him that she could
       not afford to lose the increased feed water
       production which results from having maxi-
       mum steam to the auxiliary plant (including
       evaporators) rather than to the engine throttle
       itself. (R. 4)
    b. The weather had not worsened to such a
       degree that it justified getting underway con-
       sidering the diplomatic desirability of contin-
       uing the port visit uninterrupted. (R. 17)

14. That at 0515 the port anchor chain was veered to 100
    fathoms (approximately). (R. 4) (Ex. 10-61)

15. That the starboard anchor had been made ready for
    letting go at the time 100 fathoms of chain had been
    veered to the port anchor. This "readiness" consisted
    of taking the port anchor chain from the wildcat [*the
    electric or steam capstan*], putting the port anchor on
    to the chain stopper and shifting the starboard anchor
    from the compressor to the wildcat. (R. 42)

16. That at approximately 0930, the gig [*originally a six-
    oared boat, now motorized, reserved for the Cap-
    tain's use*] carried away its moorings at the boom
    and began to drift down the ship towards the beach.
    The gig was recovered off the fantail as it drifted by.
    The gig was subsequently sent to the beach for safe
    keeping by the beach guard which had been posted
    the day before on anchoring. The motor whaleboat
    was hoisted to the regular position on the starboard
    davit heads. (Ex. 12-1)

17. That during the day of Tuesday the 6th, the weather continued to worsen sufficiently to necessitate the cancellation of official calls and subsequent visits and social events aboard and ashore. (R. 3)

18. That the wind on the afternoon of the 6th continued from the southeast. Synoptic reports were regularly evaluated by the Commanding Officer and navigator. On the basis of these reports, the Commanding Officer expected a shift of wind direction as indicated above in paragraph 8 during the afternoon or evening of 6 February. (R. 5)

19. That at about 1505, with boating secured, the quarterdeck watch and watch officer shifted from the quarterdeck to the bridge in order to better enable the watch to keep track of the ship's position. (R. 42)

20. That rounds of bearings were logged and plotted at intervals varying from 18 to 40 minutes during the time frame of 1505-1800. Testimony indicated that instructions were given on the afternoon of 6 February which required bearings to be taken at 10 minute intervals. The bearing book and other testimony indicates that this instruction was never implemented. There is some evidence that rounds of bearings other than those logged could have been taken. (R. Ex. 11, 4)

21. That the bridge watch officer standing the 1600-2000 watch had not taken and plotted bearings personally during the course of his watch. He had, however, selected two ranges of 2 points each ashore which he had used to mentally check the ship's position during the course of his duties. He had last visually checked these ranges and found them satisfactory some time

prior to 1745. These ranges had become obscure as darkness fell approaching 1800. (R. 60)

22. That the anchor watch reported the tend of the chain and degree of strain (1 o'clock, medium) between 1800 and 1830. (R. 74, 152, 162 Ex. 10)

23. That the weather was foul and it was raining intermittently during the period from 1800 onward. (R. 154, 161)

24. That the bridge watch officer, Ensign Dolan, who had the watch between 1810 (relief for the evening meal) and 1840 had been wakened from a sound sleep at 1805 and had reached the bridge at 1810 where he had relieved the watch having received little, if any, information on the ship's position and readiness that he could recall. (R. 73)

25. That the watch officer, Ensign Dolan, relieving for the evening meal was not familiar with the navigational land marks ashore and did not, himself take any bearings during his tour between 1810 and the time he was relieved at about 1840. (R. 73, 74)

26. That the watch officer, Ensign Wilson, who came back on duty at about 1840, relieved the watch without checking the ship's position and accepted a statement that the ship's position had not changed. (R. 60, 65)

27. That the last round of bearings alleged to have been plotted prior to grounding was taken and plotted by JONES, a seaman undesignated quartermaster striker, at 1800. One line of bearing, which failed to cut was rejected and the ship's position was assumed to

be the northern most intersection of the remaining three. (R. 136 to 138)

28. That Crumlish, Quartermaster of the watch, as of about 1815, reported that he took a round of bearings, by himself without recording them on paper, compared them mentally with the 1800 bearings and found them to be within satisfactory limits. He did not report that he had not plotted these bearings at about 1815 to the officer of the deck, but there is some indication that he may have indicated to the watch officer on the bridge that the comparisons were satisfactory with the 1800 bearings. (R. 113, 117)

29. That discussions with the aforementioned Quartermaster while under oath discloses that his ability to remember accurately 3 digit numbers for 30 seconds of elapsed time is subject to question and serious doubt. (R. 129)

30. That there was an officer on the bridge writing his deck log from an earlier watch at the chart desk during the period from about 1810 to 1830 whose log books improperly covered the harbor chart and the bearing book and thereby allegedly made it impossible and inconvenient to record, plot and properly compare the bearings taken by Crumlish at about 1815 with the 1800 bearings taken by Jones. (R. 113, 114)

31. That the anchor watch experienced a feeling akin to disorientation (vertigo) some time after 1800 (opinion) when, with his back to mount 51 looking forward, he lost sight of the lights ashore and saw nothing but blackness throughout his arc of vision (beam to beam). (R. 155, 156)

32.   That at the same time the anchor watch stated he experienced a distinct sensation of going backwards. He left his post on the forecastle and ran to the closest telephone (amidships) to report his "feelings." He saw white water and rocks to port; so he continued running aft to the fantail telephone to get a better look at the rocks before reporting to the bridge. He made his report. (R. 155, 156, 157)

33.   That at about the same time as the forecastle sentry and anchor watch made his report, the Commanding Officer, who was in his cabin having just finished the evening meal, sensed a new motion of the ship and ran to the bridge. (R. 5)

34.   That the ship was observed from ashore at 1830 by harbor pilot to be moving in a manner which indicated she was not intentionally underway and was being set in the direction of the breakwater. At the time of observation the ship had covered about half the distance from her normal position at anchor to the breakwater. (R. 80, 125)

35.   That the watch officer who had relieved for the evening meal at 1810 had himself been relieved at about 1840 and was below when the first bump was felt a few minutes later. (R. 134, 135)

36.   That, on feeling a bump, the Chief Engineer contacted watches in engineering spaces from his stateroom to determine whether any word had been received from the bridge. On being informed that no word had been received, the Chief Engineer ordered steam to the port engine, another boiler lit off, and preparations for answering bells. Although sea details had not been set, engineering personnel were manning their stations. (R. 87, 88)

37. That upon reaching the bridge, the Commanding Officer ordered setting of special sea details. The IMC [*shipwide announcing system*] was not used to announce the emergency. And the port engine was ordered ahead. By the time steam could be gotten to the throttle on the port engine, the port wheel could not be rotated with the jacking gear. (R. 5, 61, 88, 166)

38. That before (by the time) steering engines could be lit off and steering control shifted to the bridge, the rudder had been jammed with a considerable right angle on it. Testimony on diver's inspection revealed the rudder now lying on the bottom having sheared by the rudderpost. (R. 6)

39. That steam to the starboard engine was ordered by the Chief Engineer and after the starboard engine was ordered ahead it was rotated at maximum RPM's permitted by available steam until all boilers had to be secured. Contact with rocks so broke and ground down the blades that the starboard wheel hub is now like a sharpened pencil point with no blades on it. (R. 88, Verbal from Diver)

40. That the port screw was jammed and locked by rocks and hull even before efforts were made to turn the shaft. (Verbal from Diver)

41. That subsequent diver examination of the port screw revealed that its blades had been driven through the hull.

42. That the ship had broached onto the breakwater and was aground along her entire length when the starboard anchor was let go. The starboard anchor is located on the bottom approximately 30 feet abeam

of the starboard hawse pipe now with the chain piled on top of it. The port anchor was shifted to the wildcat and was heaved in from the initial 100 fathoms of chain to the present condition of 75 fathoms. (R. 7, 8, 29. Ex. 22)

43.   That the ship pounded increasingly heavily on the bottom along the Colonna Rocks breakwater, with her stern against the point Del Zazzaretto, which pounding opened her up from stem to stern. (R. 7)

44.   That the Commanding Officer ordered the ship ballasted completely so that she could settle on the bottom and minimize pounding. (R. 7, 8)

45.   That preparations for abandoning ship were made and the ship was ballasted to relieve pounding when efforts to get her off under own power proved fruitless. (R. 7, 8)

46.   That when rising water required securing all boilers and it was expected that the ship could break up, abandon ship was ordered and all hands except a small securing detail departed over the port side in life rafts and cleared the ship from the midships area through the opening in the Colonna Rocks breakwater about 40 yards south of the northern end. These life rafts then traveled some 500 yards through heavy surf to the beach near the front of Albergo Delle Rose. (R. 8, 9)

47.   That abandoning ship was accomplished in a most seamanlike manner under adverse conditions without loss of life or serious injury. (R. 8, 9, 32)

48.   That the port side of the ship lies along the Colonna

Rocks breakwater and is approximately 60 yards inside of the 3 fathoms curve. (R. 31, Ex. 25)

FACTS – NAVIGATION

49. That, with the prevailing and anticipated wind direction on anchoring, the nearest shoal water which presented a hazard was approximately 320 yards from the arc in which the stern of the ship would swing when riding to 100 fathom of chain. (Distance taken by plotting on Ex. 2)

50. That BACHE had the port engine on 5 minutes standby as a precautionary measure with steam to the after fire room stop, steaming on No. 4 boiler. (R. 87)

51. That there was adequate vacuum on the port condenser to permit the port engine to be used in an emergency (5 minute standby), in the prescribed 5 minute of time. (R. 90)

52. That the ship's position as she swung to anchor was fixed by lines of bearing to 4 and some times 5 prominent features whose positions provided good cuts. Bridge personnel were instructed to consider any fix falling outside a safety circle centered on the anchor, and inscribed by the navigator on the chart used for plotting fixes, as an indication of dragging anchor. This circle had a radius of 200 yards and was centered at 36° 26'38"N, Long 28° 14'01"E. (Ex. 2, Ex. 11)

53. That no specific danger bearings on fixed points ashore were prescribed. (R. 119)

54. That bearings to navigational points, selected by either the navigator or the quartermaster, were taken

periodically and some of the bearings taken were
recorded in the bearing book. (Ex. 11)

55. That the identity of a navigational feature selected
for lines of position was not properly indicated in the
bearing book. Recorded bearings and testimony indicated that the designation of these points was shifted
from time to time and occasionally confused. (R. 51)

56. That the Commanding Officer and two officers of the
deck who had the watch between 1700 and 1845
were unable to identify bearing points ashore. (R. 14,
62-64, 74, 77, 78)

57. That one of the points ashore on which bearings
were taken during daylight hours of 6 February was
a prominent, unlighted tower (St. Angelo Tower).
(R. 56)

58. That there is a flashing red navigational light 75
yards to the west of the Tower of St. Angelo which is
much more visible and readily identifiable at night
than the unlighted tower of St. Angelo — both of
which navigational marks are on the end of the St.
Angelo promontory south-southeast of BACHE's
initial anchorage. (Ex. 2, R. 57)

59. That a practice existed in BACHE wherein all bearings taken were not necessarily recorded. This practice extended to a point wherein bearing checks
would be taken and mentally compared with previous recorded bearings to see if they were close. That
the recorded bearings in the Standard Bearing Book
of the BACHE were not consistently in the proper
columns and required a true legend to be submitted
by the navigator during court proceedings. (R. 50,
113)

60. That the required frequency with which bearings were to be taken and the frequency with which they were actually taken and recorded differed in varying degree in the minds of those responsible for taking the bearings and in the minds of those responsible for the safety of the ship (watch officers). (R. 48, 139, 141, 151)

61. That the Quartermaster who had the watch during the day (there were only two in the duty section) stated that he took bearings every 20 minutes throughout the day Tuesday. He further stated that all of these bearings were recorded. He further identified the 1800 recorded bearings as the ones he had taken but had used a writer to help him jot them down. However, an examination of the standard bearing book disclosed bearings were in fact taken and recorded throughout the day after 1005 at intervals varying from 15 to 60 minutes. (R. 141)

62. That a new page had been turned in the Standard Bearing Book just prior to the grounding. At the top of the new page there appeared only the 1720 recorded bearings and the 1800 recorded bearings. (Ex. 11, R. 121)

63. That the 1800 recorded bearings plotted into four intersections many yards distant from each other and at least one of the cuts was outside of the aforementioned limited swinging circle. Quartermaster Jones testified that he rejected one of the lines which failed to cut and plotted the 1800 position as a single point where the three remaining lines crossed on his plot. (Ex. R. 136, 137, 138)

64. That, according to his statement, the leading

Quartermaster, Crumlish, took a round of bearings shortly after relieving Jones at about 1810. Although these bearings allegedly taken about 1815-1820, were not recorded or plotted, and the earlier rejected bearing was not checked, Crumlish testified that his rounds of bearings agreed, within two or three degrees, with those taken at 1800. That no further bearings were taken until after the ship had grounded. (R. 113, 117, 123)

65. That the movement of the ship from the anchorage was undetected by bridge personnel until they were alerted by the anchor watch only moments before the grounding. (R. 123)

66. That the ship grounded stern first on the breakwater north of point of Zazzaretto at about 1840 local time and was forced broadside to the wall by the combined force of winds and seas. (R. 80, 125)

67. That BACHE deployed to the Mediterranean without either of the two Yard Arm Mounted Anemometers operable. (R. 47)

68. That BACHE's hand-held anemometer was similarly inoperable, having fallen from its bulkhead bracket some time before 6 February. It has not been replaced and its repair had been declined by the tender on 27 January 1968. (R. 47)

69. That estimations of wind velocity and direction were not recorded. (No OPNAV Form 3144-1)

70. That BACHE's surface navigational radar was inoperable and had been for some time. (R. 56)

71. That fire control radars and fathometer were not

normally used to assist in navigation at anchor and were not in this case. (R. 16, 57, 126)

72. That CIC [*Combat Information Center*] was manned only with a voice communication watch. (R. 56)

73. That a drift lead was seldom used, and was not in this case. (R. 13)

FACTS ON NAVIGATION/PERSONNEL, PRACTICES, AIDS, EXPERIENCE, ETC.

74. That the Executive Officer had been navigator for 2 months during the ship's refresher training prior to deployment to the Mediterranean this cruise. (R. 170)

75. That during the time the Executive Officer was navigator, the quartermaster gang had enjoyed an additional Second and Third Class and generally more experienced talent than at present. (R. 103)

76. That BACHE has 15 officers assigned. This number was stated by the Executive Officer to be the allowed number plus an "extra." The Commanding Officer stated that when this "extra" existed, he assigned Lieutenant (junior grade) Weinberger to the full time job of navigator rather than use the Executive Officer on a part time basis. (R. 170)

77. That the ship's navigator is a Lieutenant (junior grade) United States Naval Reserve who had been the CIC [*Combat Information Center*] Officer and who has had the job of navigator for about 2 months. (R. 170)

78. That BACHE has an allowance of a Chief

Quartermaster, a First Class, a Second Class, and a Third Class. BACHE has assigned a Second Class Quartermaster, a Third Class, and a Class "A" School graduate (designated seaman striker) plus three undesignated strikers from the deck force. (R. 95, 100)

79. That the Executive Officer of BACHE stated that it is current CRUDESLANT [*Cruiser-Destroyer Force Atlantic Fleet*] practice to consider that a Second Class must necessarily be considered as fulfilling the experience level for the allowed Chief and/or First Class. Further, BACHE's Executive Officer stated that designated seaman strikers, due to critical shortages, are necessarily having to fill Third Class spaces and are counted as such. (R. 100)

80. That the Second Class Quartermaster (Crumlish), had been Second Class for just 6 months. (R. 105)

81. That one of the 6 men in the BACHE Quartermaster gang, the Class "A" School graduate, was on mess cook detail. (R. 102, 118)

82. That BACHE's inport Quartermaster watches were divided port and starboard with the Third Class and 2 undesignated seaman strikers in one section; and the Second Class and one undesignated seaman striker in the other section. (R. 116)

83. That the Quartermaster section on watch 6 February (2 men only) was divided up with the seaman on throughout the day and the Second Class on all night. The Second Class had come to the bridge, having had his dinner, and took over the watch from Seaman Jones some time shortly after 1800. (R. 116)

84. That BACHE had at least 17 experienced rated petty officers among the radarmen, sonarmen and fire controlmen, whose backgrounds and general awareness of matters relating to ranges, bearings, and relative movement made them familiar with the principles of navigation. However, BACHE had not utilized this manpower resource to augment, even temporarily, the navigation department. (R. 104)

FACTS ON TRAINING, MANPOWER AND ADMINISTRATION

85. That limited experience and talent in the ship has dictated a watch standing arrangement which provides for one qualified officer of the deck underway to be in each inport watch section. (R. 10, 111)

86. That BACHE has a watch section arrangement which provides for a deck watch officer (who may be a petty officer) for each watch section, and, during the critical period in question had 2 Ensigns as deck watch officers. Ensign Wilson had the 1600-2000 watch. Ensign Dolan was the evening meal relief (1810 to 1840). (R. 10, 59)

87. That the qualified OOD [*Officer of the Deck*] on the day of the grounding, 6 February, was Lieutenant (junior grade) Weinberger, the navigator. (R. 4)

88. That close questioning of witnesses disclosed that unanticipated emergencies were to be handled by calling the Captain and/or the OOD rather than having first hand knowledge (even though it be by instruction only), of what to do if the more experienced talent happened to be unavailable at the moment. (R. 69, 70, 79)

89. That three of the interested parties (the two watch officers and the navigator) as well as the 1600-2000 anchor watch had not been instructed as to how to tell from feeling the anchor chain, with your feet, for example, whether or not the anchor was dragging. (R. 58, 67)

90. That BACHE had dragged anchor while anchored in a port on the French Riviera a short time ago so the experience is not new to the ship and the navigator. (R. 58, 70)

91. That two young bridge watch officers, who are interested parties, were taking junior officer training courses but neither had completed many assignments. For example, Ensign Dolan had been assigned for several months but had yet to be in an engine space. (R. 77)

92. That the Executive Officer stated that he felt no obligation to oversee and supervise officer training, enlisted training and/or specifically supervision and training of the navigation department. (R. 97, 98, 101)

93. That the Executive Officer, during his testimony, disclaimed any responsibility for training, and emphasized repeatedly that he was the administrator of the ship which required over 8 hours a day at his desk. (R. 97, 98)

94. That the Executive Officer acknowledged that it was his responsibility to assign available manpower resources in the ship to those departments which needed them. (R. 97, 99)

95. That the Commanding Officer stated that personal

instruction and correction "when needed" and "as appropriate opportunity presents itself" is his preferred technique for training officers, rather than group instruction. (R. 12, 13, 164)

FACTS — MISCELLANEOUS

96. That local squalls (Siroccos) in the Rhodes anchorage are frequent at this time of year wherein winds prevail from a southerly direction. (H.O. PUBS)

97. That commercial ships caught in such squalls off Rhodes are regularly obliged to move to the western side of the island under such conditions. (H.O. PUBS)

98. That the navigational and weather hazards of Rhodes are well publicized and were known to the Commanding Officer. (R. 2)

99. That weather warnings are generally timely and was the case in this instance. (R. 5)

100. That since termination of RHN [*Royal Hellenic Navy*] control of the Port of Rhodes several years ago, anchorages are no longer assigned by port authorities. Ships arriving in the roadstead are permitted to select any anchorage which does not foul the channel or hazard ships already anchored. (R. 80)

101. That according to the statement of the Port Director, many USN and other warships previously have ridden out storms at the anchorage selected by Commanding Officer, BACHE. (R. 80, 125)

102. That an examination of the bottom at the point of initial anchorage disclosed not the mud recorded on the

chart (HO-4194) but rather a mixture of sharp edged white and black volcanic sand. (Ex. 22, R. 111)

103. That the sandy bottom of the roadstead does not constitute ideal holding ground, but the shallow depth at the point selected by BACHE permits optimum scope-to-depth ratio for destroyer types. (R. 2, 111)

104. That the bottom in the area of the initial point of anchoring as plotted by the navigator, USS BACHE (Point A, Exhibit 22) was clear with no evidence of anchor marks on 9 February 1968. (Ex. 22)

105. That the bottom at the point bearing 310 degrees T, 220 yards (Point B, Exhibit 22) from the plotted position of the USS BACHE's port anchor on 5 February 1968 (Point A, Exhibit 22) was scored by marks of the anchor flukes. (Ex. 22)

106. That the bottom in the area of point B, Exhibit 22, was marked with many parallel scores characteristic of marks caused by anchors dragging across the bottom. (Ex. 22)

107. That the area of the bottom from the present position of the USS BACHE's port anchor to Point B, Exhibit 22 is scored by marks such as an anchor's flukes would cause when the anchor dragged or tumbled across the bottom. At several locations along the scored path, intermittent deeper gouges in the bottom were in evidence, further characteristic of marks caused by an anchor tumbling as it dragged. (Ex. 22)

108. That the Points B and that labeled as "Position of port anchor after grounding" on Exhibit 22 lie along the true bearing 310 degrees from Point A (initial

plotted position of this port anchor) at distances of 220 yards and 770 yards respectively. (Ex. 22)

109. That an examination of the anchor chain from hawse pipe to anchor in its present position indicates the chain to be intact and the anchor well dug in. (Ex. 22)

FACTS — INJURIES

110. That there was no loss of life and no serious injury. Personnel with minor injuries sustained were BMC Arthur SMN ERB, USN; TN Antonio S. GALANG, USN; QM3 William A. SALYERS, USN; TN Bill M. VILLNUEVA, USN. (R. 34, 35)

SUMMARY

• *Bache* anchored in the Port of Rhodes shortly before 1000 on the morning of 5 February 1968. The wind was from the southeast, tending to strike *Bache* directly and set her toward the beach, but the wind force was not excessive, and the direction was predicted to shift from southeast to southwest. From the southwesterly wind, *Bache* would have had the protection of a lee afforded by the land mass and would have been set on a safe heading. The direction of the wind did not shift as predicted, and during the night of 5-6 February, the force increased to the extent that between 0400 to 0800 on the sixth, the navigator recommended to the Commanding Officer that the readiness of the engines be increased and the port anchor chain be veered. The port engine was on five-minute standby with steam to the after fireroom stop, steaming on number four boiler. The Commanding Officer decided to veer chain only (from 75 to 100 fathoms), because the ship had only 50% feed water on board, and he did not wish to divert steam from the auxiliary plant (including evaporators) to the engine throttle.

- During the day, Tuesday, 6 February, the wind continued from the southeast and the weather worsened. Official calls and visits were canceled. Boating was secured. At 1505 the quarterdeck watch was shifted to the bridge to permit keeping better observation of the ship's position. During the 1600-2000 watch, the bridge watch officer did not personally take and plot bearings. He selected two ranges of two points each ashore and mentally checked the ship's position by these. His last such check was at some time prior to 1745. The points ashore became obscure as darkness fell approaching 1800. The bridge watch officer was relieved for the evening meal between 1810 and 1840. The relieving officer was not informed of landmarks ashore, and did not himself check the ship's position. Upon returning at 1840 and resuming the watch, the watch officer did not check the ship's position and accepted the statement of the 1810-1840 watch officer that the position had not changed. A seaman, undesignated Quartermaster striker, plotted some bearings at about 1800. The leading Quartermaster on board, who had been Second Class for about six months, was Quartermaster of the watch. He stated that he took a round of bearings at about 1815 without recording or plotting them, and mentally compared them with the 1800 bearings. His ability to recall accurately a series of three digit numbers was not good, and the 1800 plot of recorded bearings showed four intersections many yards distant from each other, with one of the bearings having been rejected by the seaman who took it. Moreover, an officer was writing the deck log at the chart desk from 1810 to 1830, with logbooks covering the harbor chart and bearing book precluding convenient reference to those records for comparative purposes.

- At 1830, *Bache* was observed from ashore by a harbor pilot to have been set about half the distance from her previous position at anchor to the breakwater. A bump was felt aboard shortly after 1840. By the time steam could be gotten to the throttle of the port engine, the port wheel could not be rotated with the jacking gear. It later appeared that the blades of the port propeller had been driven through the hull. Before steering engines could be lit off and steering control shifted to the bridge, the rudder had been jammed with a considerable right angle on it. (The rudder was later found sheared off at the post). Steam was ordered to the starboard engine and the starboard propeller rotated, but contact with rocks completely broke off and ground down the blades. The ship broached onto the breakwater and was aground along her entire length. The ship pounded heavily on the bottom, being opened up from stem to stern. The ship was ballasted to permit her to settle on the bottom and minimize pounding. Abandoning ship was accomplished in a most seamanlike manner under adverse conditions without loss of life or serious injury. The extent of damage to the *Bache* has been considered to render it uneconomical to attempt to restore her to full service.

The skipper of the USS *Bache* was deceived by the description of the harbor bottom as a good holding ground. And he was negligent in regard to the safety of his ship in not anticipating the coming storm with accompanying wind shift and increased force. He also failed to take into account the low state of training of the crew for the coming situation and the closeness of the ship to the shore, especially when she swung. And finally, his concern with the need to run the condensers in order to provide more water for the boilers was not adequately balanced against the possibility that the ship might have to use her engines to maintain station, let alone go to emergency power to allow him to extricate the *Bache* from a precarious position.

In the naval and maritime services, the Captain is responsible for his ship and for the actions of his subordinates.

The proud USS *Bache*, having fought in several wars, like all her predecessors save the famous Revolutionary War frigates *Constellation* and *Constitution* ("Old Ironsides"), and all the battleships that have been seconded to the states whose name they bore, was cut into scrap with only her name and her pennant remaining. The destroyer could have returned to mothballing, and later to the wrecking ball. She chose, rather, to go on the rocks.

Who is to say if a ship, cold or hot iron, had not a mind, a soul, and a will. The *Bache* had proven herself different. Taking her crew with her, she had in her final voyage gained herself a place in the history books. As Ulysses mused, should "the gulfs have washed her down" or, did she, at the end, "see the Achilles whom we [*she*] knew"?

A Fatal Collision —
The USS *Wasp*
and the USS *Hobson*

ON THE spring of 1952, the United States was yet locked in a bitter struggle with North Korea. Stalemate had become the order of the day on the peninsula and there was little hope that the U.S. would once again think in terms of what to do after it had driven the Communist hordes across the Yalu River. America had her hands full keeping the Communists from taking Seoul in South Korea. The USSR was a stated adversary and always up to some mischief. For these reasons it is no surprise that the U.S. Navy would send a blacked-out Task Force, known as Task Unit 88.1, across the Atlantic to Gibraltar in the spring to rendezvous with the U.S. Sixth Fleet.

The USS *Wasp* at sea.

The USS *Hobson* in wartime paint, before conversion to a fast minesweeper.

A sister ship to the USS *Hobson*, the USS *Emmons* (DD-457) in 1943, a Bristol Class destroyer, before being converted to a destroyer-minesweeper.

The USS *Emmons* (DMS-18), a Bristol Class destroyer, after being converted to a fast minesweeper in 1945. The aft turret has been removed to add minesweeping gear.

Groups were comprised of capital ships traveling separately with their escort. Unit, 88.1.1 was comprised of the carrier *Wasp* (CV-18) and its escorts, *Rodman* (DMS-21) and *Hobson* (DMS-26), which had been converted to destroyer-minesweepers. Though both had been recommissioned as such ten years before, the ships were still capable of escorting the Navy's fastest carriers.

The *Wasp* normally traveled at 25 knots, but when called to the test, ran smoothly at 28, and in a pinch could break 30. Her escorts, which displaced 1,700 tons, each could manage 29 knots with no difficulty. The officers on the destroyers were housed in the forward compartments, while the enlisted men were in one of the four compartments in the stern.

It is fitting in naval circles, to think of an escort as being subservient; not exactly a lackey but an errand runner, a protector, and one who will take the brunt of a thrust in order to protect the grand mistress. During carrier night takeoffs and landings, the escorts, called plane guards, stood off the stern of the carrier, prepared to retrieve lost fliers — those who by misfortune plunged into the ocean during takeoff or final approach. Because of the altitude, speed, and controllability of the aircraft, it was unlikely that the aircrews would be retrieved alive, but the appearance of the ships ready to search for the fallen made it all the more seemly.

Such a scene took place the moonless night of April 26, 1952, in mid-Atlantic when the *Wasp*, an antisubmarine (ASW) support carrier, prepared to launch her planes in a night exercise.

The *Wasp* was a World War II Essex Class carrier, but she had been modernized for her new role. She was the first to have an "angled" deck, and, like the other 23 ships of the Class (except the USS *Antietam*), was 820 feet in length at the waterline, with a 120-foot beam, a draft of 31 feet, and a flight deck 96 feet above the water. She displaced 33,000 tons standard and 40,800 tons fully loaded. The *Wasp* carried two catapults and 45 aircraft, including 16 to 18 helicopters. Her four 5-inch guns accompanied an array of antiaircraft guns. Her four Westinghouse turbines would drive her at greater than 30 knots for protracted periods. Aboard were 1,615 officers and crew; a full ASW group complement comprised an additional-al 800 officers and men.

The carrier had been laid down at the Newport News, Virginia, shipyard in 1943, and had been completed and commissioned in 1944. Later, she had undergone fleet rehabilitation and modernization to improve her anti-submarine capabilities. The USS *Wasp* was decommissioned in November 1971, because of material problems, and scrapped in July 1972.

The class had been originally designated as Aircraft Carriers (CV), but in October 1952 had been renamed Support Aircraft Carriers (CVS).

The other major player in this maritime drama was the USS *Hobson*, which initially was a Benson-Livermore Class destroyer, laid down at the Charleston, South Carolina, Navy Yard in November 1940, launched in September 1941, and commissioned in January 1942. The sleek two-stacker displaced 1,700 tons, was 341 feet in length, 36 feet on the beam, and drew 18 feet. Her armament included three 5-inch guns, four 3-inchers, four 40mms, two hedgehogs, and five torpedo tubes. She developed 50,000 hp on two shafts and carried 600 tons of fuel that gave her a range of 5,000 miles.

Though all the class have been stricken from the rolls, several still serve in the navies of Greece, Italy, Turkey, and the Republic of China (Taiwan).

The USS *Hobson* had been among the group of destroyers that supported the D-Day Normandy Invasion during World War II. The flotilla *Hobson*, *Fitch*, and *Corry* were first in at Utah Beach and have the distinction of being the first naval vessels to hurl shells at the German positions. While at Omaha Beach, the *Baldwin*, *Carmick*, *Doyle*, *Emmons*, *Frankford*, *McCook*, and *Thompson* "put their bows on the bottom" as they came in to give support to the invading ground troops. This was a maneuver not sanctioned in naval navigation, as one might surmise. There was the reasonable possibility that the tide might ground the ship if it were to linger too long, bow stuck in the sand, for tides in the Channel have a fall that exceeds ten feet and retreat with incredible speed. A ship, so stuck, could not spend any time trying to extricate herself — certainly not while

Captain B. C. McCaffree, Commanding Officer of the USS *Wasp,* on the bridge.

there was work to be done — yet to ignore a slight grounding meant being shortly more firmly embedded. How embarrassing, at the ending of active hostilities, to find it necessary to signal the flotilla Commander, "My bow is stuck in the sand and repeated attempts at backing off have failed. Require assistance by a stern tow."

The USS *Wasp*, USS *Hobson*, and USS *Rodman* were traveling together under the Command of Captain Burnham C. McCaffree, the skipper of the *Wasp*. At the beginning of the maneuver that led to disaster, the three ships were traveling on a course of 102 degrees and steaming at 27 knots. It was a moonless clear night. The only illumination was that of the masthead lights of the three ships. The *Rodman* was 3,000 yards off the port bow, and the *Hobson* was 1,000 yards off the starboard stern. An eight-knot wind from the west (about 282 degrees) was driving four-foot swells.

The carrier launched her planes and then set about a maneuver, which when complete would put the *Wasp* on course 282 degrees, at the proper wind to land her planes. The *Rodman* and the *Hobson* were positioned to serve as tenders during plane retrieval.

In addition to Captain McCaffree on the bridge of the *Wasp* were Commander Francis Drake, the Executive Officer; Lieutenant Robert T. Herbst, Officer of the Deck; Lieutenant Page Ingraham, Junior Officer of the Deck (JOOD); Ensign Thomas Walbridge, Junior Officer of the Watch (JOOW); Harold Zigler, engine room telegraph; George Foster, Quartermaster; Norman Armstrong, helmsman; A. Y. Frank, Boatswain's Mate of the watch; Donald P. Bates, messenger; Donald Wagner, lee helmsman; and Daniel Childers and Donald Smith, circuit talkers.

On the *Hobson* bridge were the Captain, Lieutenant Commander William Tierney; Lieutenant William A. Hoefer, Jr., OOD; Lieutenant Junior Grade Donald E. Cummings, JOOD; Iredoll Proffer, messenger; Raymond Parks, navigating Quartermaster; Harry Pars, Quartermaster of the watch; R. N. Wasilkowski, bridge talker; Albert Desrosiers, Boatswain's Mate of the watch; Paul E. Iseman, helmsman; Ralph Painter, engine order telegraph; Samuel Craver, Quartermaster First Class; and George Swan, Mineman 3. Of her crew of 240, more than 150 were asleep in the darkened stern compartment.

Lieutenant Commander William Joseph Tierney, Commander of the USS *Hobson*, was 32 years of age the night of April 26, 1952, when he met the USS *Wasp* in death-dealing circumstance. Born in Philadelphia, he had attended the prestigious St. Joseph Preparatory School, from which he had graduated in 1937. Following summer vacation, he had matriculated

Commander William J. Tierney of the USS
Hobson.

to the Pennsylvania State
Nautical School in the
fall and had graduated
two years later with an
Associate Degree as a
Nautical Deck Officer.
He immediately re-
ceived the appointment
as a Merchant Marine
Cadet on April 29, 1939.

To while away the time
until the inevitable call came,
Tierney had joined the United
States Line Company as Third Offi-
cer and then Second Officer. In early
1942, the awaited call from the U.S. Navy made him an Ensign in the
Reserve, to rank from March 12, 1941. He had reported for active duty in
January 1942 and had been assigned immediately to the store ship USS
Pastories (AF-16). Tierney had served as a watch and battery officer for a
year. He then had become the navigator, the duty that he had held until
spring of 1944 when he had become navigator of the cargo ship USS
Alshain until December of 1945. During his last month aboard, he had
commanded the *Alshain*.

In early 1946, Tierney had become first a temporary Commander and
then Commander of the passenger ship USS *Crosley* (APD 87). During the
Philippine Islands liberation in late 1944, early 1945, the *Crosley* was one
of the vessels that had landed troops of the invasion, being part of the U.S.
Seventh Fleet. Tierney had taken a minor shrapnel wound during the landing in Lingayen Gulf, though it had not been incapacitating and had not
relegated him to shore. He had received the Philippine Liberation Medal
and the Purple Heart for his action. He had remained aboard the *Crosley*
as Commander until the summer of 1946, at which time he had reverted to

Reserve status and took an assignment as a deck officer in the Merchant Marine.

For his entire career at sea, William Tierney had longed to command a fighting ship in the U.S. Navy. From talking to or corresponding with friends yet on active duty, he had learned that many of the sleek World War II destroyers' aft decks had been cleared of guns and depth charges, in order to go back into service as minesweepers. Tierney was hopeful that should he return to active duty, he would receive command of such a ship.

He was rewarded by being assigned as the Executive Officer of an Atlantic Fleet destroyer for two assignments in the Mediterranean Sea. By the fateful night in April 1952, Tierney had been in a Command less than two months, had been at sea in the *Hobson* less than two weeks, and had *never* practiced in daylight what he was ordered to do that night, under conditions of absolute blackout.

At 2210, the *Wasp* sent the signal "FOX CORPEN 265, TACKLINE FOX SPEED 27," which was acknowledged by both plane guards. At 2221, the turn-and-speed signal was executed. When the turn-and-speed signal was received, Lieutenant Commander Tierney took over the conn of the *Hobson* and retained it until the time of the collision. At 2220 the carrier had sent the message, "TURN 260 TACKLINE SPEED 27," which had been receipted by both plane guards.

At the execution of the maneuver, the USS *Wasp* turned starboard (right), with a turning radius of 1,500 yards at 27 knots. During the turn, Captain McCaffree determined that the course of 260 degrees, which he had prescribed, would not be suitable for retrieval and upon arriving at 258 degrees the *Wasp* sent the second message, "MIKE CORPEN 250." Interestingly, neither plane guard acknowledged the signal. It was not heard by anyone on the bridge of the *Rodman*, nor by any of the survivors of the *Hobson*.

To understand properly the situation at the beginning of the maneuver, it is necessary to recount the scene, the ocean conditions, and the plans to execute the change in position.

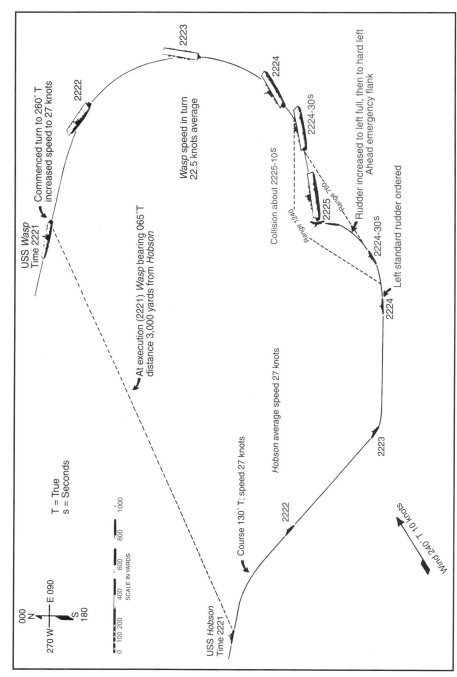

The approximate sequence of positions of the USS *Wasp* and the USS *Hobson* from the commencement of the turn until the time of collision, April 26, 1952. From the Court of Inquiry transcript diagram.

The three ships in the dark were all steaming on a course of 102 degrees at 27 knots — the carrier *Wasp* the principal, with the destroyers *Rodman* 3,000 yards off its port bow and *Hobson* 1,000 yards to starboard off the stern. From these positions they were to make simultaneous moves in order to place the Task Force on the course of 282 degrees.

To do this, the *Wasp* chose to perform a sweeping turn to starboard. The *Rodman* had but to stay outside of the carrier, and turn either to port or starboard and take up the new course of 282 degrees at 3,000 yards from the *Wasp*. Her main concern was to slacken her speed properly in order to pull astern of the *Wasp* and then resume full speed once the carrier had come to proper position.

With the *Hobson* it was not so simple. If she had stayed on her present course, she would have collided with the carrier as it turned. She, therefore, had to change her course. First, she chose to alter course to 130 degrees, to get outside the carrier's turn. Had these two courses been allowed to reach a conclusion, the destroyer would have passed the carrier port to port. Once this passing had been accomplished, the destroyer would have had to race to reach her new station, and the carrier could have graciously slowed down to allow her to do so.

The *Hobson's* other option was to turn to port at once when the carrier began her starboard turn. By calculating the final position of the *Wasp*, the *Hobson* had only to clear the carrier and turn up the horses.

Instead, Commander Tierney, for whatever reason, chose to make an intricate maneuver and pass close, port to port, and then, once clear, to turn sharply to port and pass astern of the carrier. How he then chose to catch up with the carrier is another matter.

Tierney's change of course was predicated on the dictum of the Task Force Commander:

AN ESCORT, NOT IN POSITION, SERVES NO USEFUL PURPOSE, AND THEREFORE SHOULD EXPEDITE GETTING ON STATION, EVEN AT THE EXPENSE OF AN *OCCASIONAL MISTAKE*.

Though Commander Tierney had more than two years experience as the Executive Officer (EXO) of a destroyer, on the *Hobson* — a destroyer-minesweeper — he had been in Command only five weeks and at sea but a week, three and one-half days of which had been spent with the Task

Group. The maneuver about which this tale revolves had never been done before by the members of the Task Group, and this very maneuver, to be executed under blackout conditions, has been thought to carry risk and *should have been practiced under daylight conditions.*

On the bridge on Saturday night, April 26, 1952, the skipper, Lieutenant Commander Tierney, his Executive and Officer of the Watch Lieutenant Hoefer, and the helmsman Iseman and Boatswain's Mate Desrosiers all awaited the order from the *Wasp* to take up plane-guard station during the execution of a sweeping turn, which would reverse their present course.

As recited in later testimony, upon receiving the order, Tierney asked Hoefer what he would do to effect the change of station. Hoefer replied that he would come right with ten degrees of rudder and slow down until the *Wasp* had completed her turn and caught up with the *Hobson*. Then, when the carrier had passed her, starboard to port, she would resume speed to allow her to equal that of the *Wasp*.

Tierney would have none of this staid and sensible means of getting into position. He explained to Hoefer that he intended to take station in "a destroyer-like fashion" and explained his plan. The *"occasional mistake,"* which he had been "granted" by the *Wasp,* gave Tierney assurance that while he conducted the maneuver this boon would prevail should he commit some glaring error that he would be called upon to explain. Tierney then told Hoefer his plan, which caused Hoefer to immediately try to dissuade the Commander from what appeared to be a dangerous venture.

Tierney's plan was that the *Hobson* respond to the starboard turn of the *Wasp* by changing her course to 130 degrees true at 27 knots, ostensibly to put her OUTSIDE the turning circle of the carrier, and to allow her the freedom of maneuverability to complete the following course changes, which were to bring her to the *Wasp's* starboard stern.

Hoefer's objection was that in turning but slightly from the "position to be" of the *Wasp*, the *Hobson,* during the maneuver, would be closing the carrier at the combined speed of 56 knots. If the escort made adjustments, and the ships were to pass, port-to-port, the distance between them would be less than 500 yards — too close in Hoefer's book.

After setting his mind to make the repositioning, Tierney, now fiery toward his second in Command, positioned himself on the flying bridge and gave the fatal series of orders from the starboard wing.

The helmsman, a surviver of the coming collision, testified that after the change to 130 degrees, Tierney gave a series of course changes, which the helmsmen described as "Go right, Go left, Go right." Time was running out for the *Hobson*.

At 2222, the two ships were in approximately the same relative positions as they had been when traveling together at 065 degrees. A minute later, at 2223, the *Hobson*, on her new course, found her sister ship well into her starboard turn. At this time, the *Hobson* turned port to approximately 090 degrees. One minute later, at 2224, the vessels were 1,500 yards apart and, barring change in course, would pass port-to-port at 500 yards, at which time the *Hobson* would pass astern of the *Wasp* and try to catch up.

However, according to the Court of Inquiry transcript, Lieutenant Commander Tierney had assumed incorrectly that the *Wasp's* tactical turning diameter was 1,200 yards, instead of the 1,500 yards.

Tierney then ordered left standard rudder — a course that would put him *squarely across the bow of the carrier*. The reader must realize that before this time, 2224, the ships were not *in extremis* and any dereliction of duty, which was to be later found, *must have occurred after this time*.

After the fateful order to course 090 degrees, the helmsman, P. E. Iseman, later testified that Tierney never steadied on a course, but kept trying to come closer to the carrier. Perhaps Tierney was thinking his lack of superior speed would make it impossible to catch up with the *Wasp* unless he passed her close by and then went *immediately* under her stern.

Ensign D. D. Lane, in the Combat Information Center of the *Hobson*, shouted up to the bridge via the voice tube, "Lost contact due to short range. Do we intend to pass astern?"

This query from down below suddenly awakened Tierney to the terrible deadly mistake he had made. His very last command was "Left full rudder. Hard left. All ahead emergency flank!" Though the conn had been taken from Hoefer by Tierney, after Tierney gave his last command Hoefer shouted, "Stand by for collision!"

Immediately before the collision occurred, Boatswain's Mate Desrosiers shouted, "Abandon ship!"

Seaman Harry Rapp, Quartermaster of the watch remembers seeing the bow of the *Wasp* towering over the bridge. "Then we hit," he was to testify. The time was 2225.

After the collision, Desrosiers and Iseman — still on the bridge — had the following conversation. Iseman, having regained his feet after the shock of the impact, shouted to Desrosiers, "She's listing bad. Do you think she'll right herself?"

"No," shouted Desrosiers. "Let's get out of here!"

They both then climbed through the windows of the pilothouse, out onto the listing hull, and swam away into the sea before she sank. Both survived.

On the bridge of the *Wasp* no one had viewed with alarm the position nor the movements of the *Hobson*, for it was thought that although she was closing at the combined speeds of both ships, her intention was to pass port-to-port and then cross astern of the carrier.

At 2224, the ships had been separated by 1,500 yards, on a course to pass comfortably though close. Tierney had given the order of "left standard rudder," which in one minute would spell doom for his ship. Almost immediately, those of the *Wasp*'s bridge could make out the approaching masthead lights and came to realize that the *Hobson* was about to collide — but where was uncertain.

The bridge of the *Hobson* was the first place where the danger was realized. Tierney by then had sensed his mistake. Hoefer, the deck officer of the *Hobson* who survived, testified that he saw the large carrier without binoculars at over 3,000 yards. Herbst, deck officer of the *Wasp*, testified that he could see the small ship clearly without binoculars and had no indication of its turn to the left. Hence there could be no evasion, because the *Hobson*'s turn came as a complete surprise to those on the *Wasp*, who could not have recognized the danger until less than 30 seconds before the collision.

Testimony was given that after being warned of the danger, at 2224+30 seconds, Commander Tierney ordered "full left," then seconds later, "hard left," then "full flank." The latter order was recorded as his last utterance on earth.

Captain McCaffree, aboard the *Wasp*, watched in utter disbelief as the *Hobson* bore down from the port quarter and disappeared beneath the *Wasp*'s bow. He gasped as her bow appeared to starboard, but was momentarily hopeful as her funnels appeared. However, his view of the *Hobson* was prelude to the shuddering crash felt throughout the great ship as she struck the smaller vessel, cut her in half, and continued past the sinking separated portions of the wreck. McCaffree immediately ordered full astern and the casting overboard of life-saving equipment. Within five minutes the first boat from the *Wasp* was in the water searching for survivors. Lights from the carrier began to illuminate the scene.

The stern of the destroyer, where many of the off-duty crew had been asleep, was the first to sink; thus there were very few survivors. One can but imagine the few moments of terror as the shock of the collision sent everything tumbling about. Then water rushed inward as the *Hobson* sank. No one in their bunks in the aft portion had been wearing a life preserver — those few rescued were found clinging to flotation devices dropped by the *Wasp*.

The majority of survivors came from the forward portion of the *Hobson* — it had remained afloat longer. Lieutenant Hoefer later testified that after the collision he clung to the port rail of the listing ship. He was soon in the water, along with Commander Tierney and Lieutenant (JG) Cummings and Quartermaster Parks. As the water rose, it was apparent that should they survive, they must take to the water and swim away. Hoefer, Parks, and Cummings swam and found life preservers, which had been dropped by the *Wasp*. They were saved.

Hoefer testified that it was only later after rescue that he had become aware that Commander Tierney could not swim. Tierney was clinging to the submerged rail of the bridge, still wearing his parka and his binoculars, when Hoefer last saw him.

The sister escort, the *Rodman*, joined in the search. Survivors, when located were hoisted aboard the nearest of the two ships. After midnight, Captain McCaffree concluded that all survivors had been found and that he should attend to his planes, which were circling and low on fuel. He abandoned the search to the *Rodman*. His decision proved correct, for no survivors were found after he broke off.

Crewmen of the USS *Wasp* look on as the few survivors of the USS *Hobson* are taken aboard.

After the collision, the propeller shaft, lodged in the bow of the USS *Wasp*, was all that remained of the USS *Hobson*.

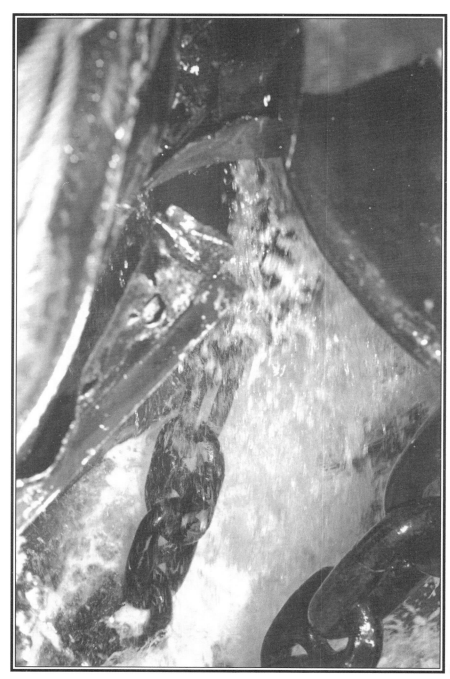

The port and starboard anchor chains hang out through the bow of the USS *Wasp*, after the collision with the USS *Hobson*.

With dawn came the wind, which had dispersed the oil slick, and all that remained were numerous life jackets from the *Wasp*. Finally, the destroyers — by then three — were ordered to abandon the search.

The *Wasp*, her bow torn so badly that she could not make forward movement without flooding herself, turned stern first and began her long return to Boston. It was a torturous voyage. Several times during the first days, when the seas were yet high, the carrier began to yaw and could not be righted until a full circle had been made. With the arrival of calm seas, Captain McCaffree stopped and put out boats to inspect the damage. The gash in the bow was 15 feet from top to bottom and 90 feet in length. Twelve feet of the opening were below the waterline. The tendency to yaw was attributed to the 600 feet of anchor chain, which the *Wasp* was dragging. One broken propeller shaft from the sunken *Hobson* protruded from the bow of the *Wasp*.

With the death of Commander Tierney, no one would ever know his thinking on the change of course. As always, the barn door is closed after the horse is out. Immediately following the collision, the U.S. Navy issued instructions that whenever possible, escorts would take plane station BEFORE changing course to launch and that launch with escorts would NOT be undertaken under blackout condition unless first having been practiced in daylight.

Of the *Hobson's* crew of 240, only 61 survived. Only one body had been recovered; all others lost went down with the sinking of the two halves of the ship.

The U.S. Navy Court of Inquiry met in New York and concluded by assigning the blame to Commander Tierney, but citing Captain McCaffree and Lieutenant Herbst (*Wasp* deck officer) as negligent. The president of the court, Rear Admiral Osborne B. Hardison, however, disagreed with the conclusion, attributing no blame to the latter two and fixing sole blame on

Captain Tierney. Review of the findings of the court confirmed Admiral Hardison's opinion. The full findings of the court and the writings of Hardison follow as they appear in the record of the Court of Inquiry.

**Transcript of "Opinion" and
"Review" of Court of Inquiry**

OPINION

1. That the chronological sequence of events leading up to the collision between the U.S.S. WASP (CV-19) and the U.S.S. HOBSON (DMS-26) was as follows:

    (a) A right turn by Carrier Unit 88.1.1 to 260°T [*True*] from 102°T, and speed increase from 25 to 27 knots, were properly ordered by the OTC [*Officer in Tactical Command*] in WASP, and receipted for by the HOBSON and the U.S.S. RODMAN (DMS-21) at approximately 2220, and the execution was properly sent and receipted for at 2221.

    (b) This turn was not appreciably different from that indicated in a previous information signal, sent at about 2210, which gave estimated recovery course of 265°T, and speed 27 knots; so that ample time was available for the HOBSON to plan the change of plane guard position required of her.

    (c) The original plan of the Commanding Officer of the HOBSON in the execution of the turn signal was to go to 27 knots, and to make an initial right turn from 102°T to 130°T, followed by a left turn to recovery course when WASP bore about 010°T.

    (d) The above plan was abandoned by the Commanding Officer of the HOBSON after steadying for a short time on 130°T, at which time he executed a series of brief course alterations, on an average course of about 090°T, prior to making a final sharp left turn to about 348°, which turn placed the HOBSON squarely across the bow of the WASP, which was then heading about 258°T.

(e)   The WASP commenced a standard right turn to 260°T at 2221, in accordance with signal, executed it properly, came to course 261°T, then was coming left using about seven degrees rudder to adjust course to 250°T, and was on heading about 258°T when the collision occurred.

(f)   The order to adjust course to 250°T was given by the Commanding Officer of the WASP during the original turn to 261°T, at the time WASP had reached a heading of about 258°T, and this order was passed personally by the Commanding Officer over the primary tactical circuit microphone as MIKE CORPEN 250.

(g)   The primary tactical circuit was not in use during the night maneuvers, due to a faulty primary transmitter in RODMAN, and the MIKE CORPEN signal was not passed over the secondary tactical circuit, which was in use; and since no one in the RODMAN nor any survivors of the HOBSON heard MIKE CORPEN 250, it is not believed that the Commanding Officer of the HOBSON heard the MIKE CORPEN signal.

(h)   The HOBSON had already entered her final left turn about the time the Commanding Officer of the WASP spoke the MIKE CORPEN signal into the primary tactical circuit microphone, and it is believed that even if the signal had been received by the Commanding Officer of the HOBSON, it would not, at that time, have affected his manner of expediting the evolution.

2.   That the sequence of events, the simultaneous tracks, headings and times of the two ships were as shown on the following attached diagram marked "X."

3.   That the maneuver into the wind for the Carrier Unit was a normal maneuver, properly ordered, and could have been safely executed.

4.   That the left turn of the HOBSON across the bow of the WASP was the direct cause of the collision.

5.   That in making his final left turn, the Commanding Officer of the HOBSON committed a grave error in judgment.

6. That the ships during this maneuver were governed, as they approached positions where a risk of collision might become a possibility, by Article 27, International Rules of the Road, which states:

    "General Prudential Rule, Article 27: In obeying these rules due regard shall be had to all dangers of navigation and collision, and to any special circumstances which may render a departure from the above rules necessary in order to avoid immediate danger."

    This case is not considered to be an "end on, or nearly end on," situation, Article 18, or a "crossing" situation, Article 19, due to the short ranges, and to the speeds and course changes required in the signaled maneuver.

    The sudden left turn of the HOBSON, at about 2224, placed both ships in extremis.

7. That the evolution originally planned by the Commanding Officer of the HOBSON to reach his new station during the maneuver of the formation to recovery course, involved unnecessary and considerable risk, and was in violation of governing directives, as set forth hereinafter in paragraph 12.

8. That the HOBSON was not turning with any definite tactical diameter during her evolution leading up to the collision.

9. That in this case, the Commanding Officer of the HOBSON could have predicted the position of the WASP throughout her turn with a good degree of accuracy.

10. That in this case, the Commanding Officer of the WASP could not predict the course and speed of the HOBSON in proceeding to her assigned plane guard station.

11. That the message from Commander Screen Unit 88.1.4 (Commander Destroyer Flotilla Four) influenced the Commanding Officer of the HOBSON to endeavor to expedite his evolution.

12. That Lieutenant Commander Tierney, Commanding Officer of the HOBSON, was derelict in his duties in that he failed to

comply with U.S. Navy Regulations, Articles 0701 and 0751, which assign the Commanding Officer responsibility for the safety of his ship and for the observance of every precaution prescribed by law (including naval instructions) to prevent collision on the high seas, in the following respects:

(a) Violation of Article 27, International Rules of the Road (General Prudential Rule).

(b) Violation of Article 22, International Rules of the Road. The HOBSON, though directed by the Rules of the Road to keep out of the way of the other vessel did not do so, but crossed ahead.

(c) Violation of Article 23, International Rules of the Road. The HOBSON did not slacken her speed, stop or reverse.

(d) Violation of ATP 1, Article 533. The HOBSON, a small ship, hampered the movements of the WASP, a large ship.

(e) Violation of USF 2, Article 478(a) and (c). The HOBSON hampered the movements of WASP; crossed the bow of the WASP when it was not safe; changed a clear situation into an awkward one by lack of timely indication to others of her intent, and through an impatient haste to accomplish her evolution.

(f) Violation of USF 4, Article 924. The HOBSON attempted to cross ahead of, and turned towards instead of away from the WASP.

13. That the above derelictions of duty by Lieutenant Commander Tierney were due to poor judgment, which in turn was due principally to:

(a) His inexperience in command of DD type vessels, and in particular his lack of experience in the HOBSON, command of which he had held only about five weeks, during which time she had been at sea only about 7 days, of which only 3½ days were spent with a Task Group.

(b) His confusion at a critical time, when he changed left from course 130°T, and his complete loss of grasp of the rapidly moving tactical situation, as a result of the following factors:

(1) Night, with ships darkened, except for visible red truck lights.

(2) High closing rate of the two ships brought about by high speeds and by HOBSON's generally 090° headings.

(3) His desire to effect a rapid change in station.

(4) His incorrect assumption of a tactical diameter of 1200 yards for WASP, instead of the 1500 she was using.

14. That the derelictions of duty on the part of Lieutenant Commander Tierney were the direct cause of the collision.

15. That the reason for the final left turn of the HOBSON, which led to the collision, is difficult of explanation; however, these three possible explanations are offered for this action on the part of Lieutenant Commander Tierney:

(a) That becoming completely confused, and having lost the tactical picture, he mistakenly continued to believe that he could turn left into position, and so ordered, "left rudder."

(b) That after starting this evolution, he decided against his planned final left turn, without informing any one, and really intended to turn right instead; which in fact would have placed him near his intended position; but that he inadvertently ordered "left rudder," intending to order "right rudder." That he only became conscious of his error when, from the wing of the bridge, he observed his ship's head swinging left and he then felt it was too late to avoid a collision except by accelerating his left turn and speed, for which he gave the proper orders.

(c) That he made, through inexperience, an error in his estimate of the target angle or course, or both, of the WASP, turned left to clear her, and thereby placed his ship in extremis.

16. The maneuver in which the collision occurred involved, for the HOBSON, one of the more difficult evolutions that is required of a plane guard destroyer; namely, one that involved a change on the guide from one station to another station, closer to the guide, during a countermarch maneuver, at the beginning of which the ship is astern of the guide, and which, in this case, required of the HOBSON changes of course and speed on a dark night, with ships darkened except for visible red truck lights, and at high formation speed with no reserve speed immediately available.

17. That there was no dereliction or negligence in duty in this collision on the part of Lieutenant William A. Hoefer, Jr., 274572/1108, U.S. Naval Reserve, officer of the deck of the U.S.S. HOBSON (DMS-26).

18. That Captain McCaffree, Commanding Officer of the WASP, was negligent in his duties, in that he failed to comply with U.S. Navy Regulations, Articles 0611 and 0701, which assign him, respectively, responsibility, as senior officer present, for the safety of ships in company; and responsibility, as Commanding Officer, for the safety of his entire command. This option as to negligence is based on the following factors, in that he:

    (a) As senior officer present, in planning and in executing the maneuver which led to the collision:

        (1) Ordered a maneuver at high speed at night, with ships darkened except for red truck lights, which maneuver had not been rehearsed in daylight by ships who were in company for the first time that day, and which required an evolution by HOBSON that involved risk of collision;

        (2) Prescribed a speed for the maneuver that left no immediately available reserve speed for HOBSON above the maximum speed required for the night;

        (3) In view of the foregoing, might well have been more prudent, by ordering HOBSON (and RODMAN) to recovery stations in advance of executing the turn to recovery course, and as an extra precaution, by prescribing the use of running lights until he saw that

evolutions involved in a turn maneuver of this magni-
tude and speed were being safely executed; and

(4) Failed to comply with International Rules of the Road
by not having due regard to all risks of collision.

(b) As Commanding Officer:

(1) Assumed the HOBSON had turned right initially at
the execution of "Turn 260°T/Speed 27", and therefore, that everything was proceeding normally in execution of the signaled maneuver.

(2) Was not alert, as WASP was turning to course 260°T,
the risk of collision inherent in the position of HOB-
SON, was approximately 1 minute prior to collision,
bore about 090° relative, and was: on a course unknown to him, but actually about 090°T; at a range
unknown to him; but actually about 500 yards; and at
a closing relative speed unknown to him, but actually
about 50 knots. True bearings and ranges, if taken in
the WASP, would have given him an indication of the
HOBSON's evolvements.

(3) Commenced executing an adjustment of course of ten
degrees to the left, toward the HOBSON, without as-
certaining the position of the HOBSON, which then
bore about 345° relative from the WASP, distant about
1250 yards, and on an opposite course at high speed.
True bearings and ranges, if taken in WASP, should
have indicated a delay in this adjustment of course.

(4) Failed to comply with International Rules of the Road,
not: having due regard to all risks of collision (Article
27); preliminary – Part IV); and not keeping his course
(Article 21).

19. That Captain McCaffree, when he sighted the HOBSON in her
final left turn just prior to the collision, took quick and correct
action, in conformity with his responsibilities under Article 27,
International Rules of the Road.

20. That Captain McCaffree's seamanship after the collision in carrying out search and rescue, in recovery of planes with comparatively low wind conditions across the flight deck, and in bringing his damaged ship safely into port, was of the highest order.

21. That Lieutenant Herbst, Officer of the Deck of the WASP, was negligent in his duties, in that he failed to comply with U.S. Navy Regulations, Articles 1006 and 1010, which assign the officer of the deck responsibility for the safety of the ship, for taking immediate action to minimize any damage that might occur when there is danger of collision, and for thoroughly familiarizing himself with the laws to prevent collision and strictly complying with them. This opinion as to negligence is based on the following factors, in that he:

   (a) Expected the HOBSON would get on the port side of the WASP (the guide in the maneuver) and then turn (right) to get into plane guard station number two, and had the impression the HOBSON had carried out the signaled maneuver by simply slowing and turning (to 260°T): and, based on these beliefs, had not:

      (1) Observed the HOBSON through binoculars from about the time of execute "Turn 260°T/Speed 27" (about 4 minutes prior to collision), until after he had given orders to come left to 250°T from a heading of about 260°T, at which time the HOBSON was in a left turn towards the WASP, which resulted, approximately 50 seconds thereafter, in the collision.

      (2) Taken, or caused to be taken, true bearings of, or ranges to, the HOBSON, which approximately 1 minute prior to collision, as WASP was completing a turn to course 260°T: bore about 350° relative from the WASP; was on a course unknown to him, but actually about 090°T; was at a range unknown to him, but actually about 1300 yards; and was at a closing relative speed, unknown to him, but actually about 50 knots. True bearings and ranges, if taken in the WASP, would have given him an indication of the HOBSON's movements.

(b) Through inexperience with night recovery operations, was not alert to the danger of collision that existed in the actual circumstances; was somewhat influenced in this state of mind by the presence of the Commanding Officer in a position where the latter customarily took the conn for recovery operations, which were pending, and therefore was belatedly aware, in circumstances wherein seconds were vital, of the HOBSON's fatal left turn; and became aware of this left turn at a time when WASP was in extremis and just before the Commanding Officer assumed the conn by ordering emergency backing.

(c) Failed to comply with International Rules of the Road by not:

(1) Having due regard to all dangers of navigation and collision (Article 27).

(2) Carefully watching the compass bearing of an approaching vessel (Preliminary – Part IV).

22. That the deaths and injuries, resulting from the collision between the WASP and HOBSON, were not due to the intent of any person in the naval service.

23. That no persons other than Lieutenant Commander Tierney, whose actions were the direct cause of the collision, and Captain McCaffree and Lieutenant Herbst, both of whom were negligent in some degree, are in any way responsible for the collision.

24. That all deaths suffered, and all injuries sustained, by naval personnel as a result of the collision between the WASP and the HOBSON occurred in the line of duty and not as the result of their own misconduct.

25. That there is confusion as to the exact meaning of "MIKE CORPEN" i.e., whether it is to be used as a signal meaning, "It is necessary to adjust course to" as indicated in ATP 1, Art. 1522(c), or whether it means, "My course is," as indicated in ACP 175, page 7-8.

26. That there is room for confusion as to the meaning of the FOX

flag "at the dip," when the FOX flag is "close up," from "at the dip," ATP 1, Article 532(a) states that a carrier has the right of way when showing a signal to indicate that she is launching or recovering aircraft, while Article 1506(a) states the same right of way without mentioning a signal, but refers to Article 532(a). Article 1508(a), which gives the FOX flag signals, does not have one meaning "I am launching or recovering aircraft," but gives the meaning of "FOX close up" as, "Am operating aircraft."

27. That search and rescue operations were prompt and adequate.

28. That all persons afloat and on flotation gear, after the HOBSON sank, were picked up during search and rescue operations.

29. That there were no cases, in firm evidence, of exceptionally meritorious conduct of personnel in WASP or HOBSON during the collision, but that the senior surviving officer of the HOBSON is investigating through the Bureau of Personnel the possibility of heroism on the part of one member of the HOBSON's crew who was lost in the collision.

30. That the condition of combat readiness of the WASP was good.

31. That the condition of combat readiness of the HOBSON was satisfactory, giving consideration to the fact that about one-half her crew had recently come aboard, and most of these had served only a short time in the Navy.

32. That the conditions of material readiness of the WASP and HOBSON were good.

33. That no material, mechanical or electronic failures in the WASP, or in the HOBSON, contributed to, or caused the collision.

34. That there were no errors in the master gyrocompass or bridge repeaters of the WASP and HOBSON.

35. That there were no errors in the bridge clocks of the WASP and HOBSON, or other clocks on board those ships that might have affected maneuvering.

I agree with the findings, opinions, and recommendations of the court except in the following respects:

FACTS

I disagree with paragraph 51 of the court's findings only because I think it is superfluous. A similar statement, based on his testimony can be made with respect to Lieutenant Hoefer, OD of the HOBSON, and various other officers on the bridge of the WASP and HOBSON.

OPINION

1. I disagree with paragraph 4 of the court's opinions because I believe the left turn of the HOBSON across the bow of the WASP is not only the "direct," but the sole cause of the collision. The word "direct" should be deleted.

2. I disagree with paragraph 6 of the court's opinions for the following reasons:

   (a) The ships during the maneuver were governed by all applicable rules of the road, not solely Article 27.

   (b) When the HOBSON changed her course to the left she was not "in extremis" and she did develop a "crossing situation," which of course, passed quickly into a condition of "extremis."

3. I disagree with paragraph 12 of the court's opinions because it omits reference to Article 19, International Rules of the Road, which I consider Lieutenant Commander Tierney likewise violated. In agreeing to paragraph 7 of the court's opinions, the agreement assumed paragraph 12 to be amended to include violation of Article 19, International Rules of the Road.

4. I disagree with paragraph 14 of the court's opinions because I believe the derelictions of duty on the part of Lieutenant Commander Tierney were not only the "direct," but the sole cause of the collision. The word "direct" should be deleted.

5. I disagree with paragraph 16 of the court's opinions because I think the maneuver ordered was a routine one, used frequently, and not difficult if performed properly. I agree the maneuver became difficult when Lieutenant Commander Tierney decided to perform his evolution in a hazardous and intricate manner. Had he turned right and dropped back, using any one of several ways to close distance, it would have been simple. There was no requirement that the HOBSON change station at any particular time, before or during the turn, nor was any counter-march ordered. The signal "TURN 260° SPEED 27" called only for a simple simultaneous right turn of 158°.

6. I disagree with paragraph 17 of the court's opinions because I consider it unnecessary. As stated in paragraph 4 above, I do not consider anyone except Lieutenant Commander Tierney responsible for the collision.

7. I disagree, in general, with paragraph 18 of the court's opinions because:

    (a) Negligence on the part of Captain McCaffree is not supported by any finding of fact, nor by the evidence.

    (b) There is no <u>causal connection</u> between the collision and any of the so-called acts of negligence charged by the majority of the court against Captain McCaffree, nor does the opinion of the majority allege any such causal connection.

    (c) Specifically I disagree with paragraph 18 of the court's opinions in the following respects: (Note: For easy reference the following paragraphs carry the same numbers as do the paragraphs in the court's opinions to which they refer.)

        (a) (1) The maneuver ordered was a simple turn into the wind, with only one plane guard required to shift station, and only the carrier and the two plane guards present. Air operations had been successfully conducted in the afternoon preceding the collision, and during the night launch. The same signals and procedures were used in all cases, and the only difference in the night recovery maneuvers was the fact that HOBSON was required to change her station for the recovery. This change of station could have been executed simply and easily, with no risk of collision whatsoever. The maneuver is performed repeatedly with no rehearsal. No particular risk of collision was involved, other than that inherent in any simple maneuver. Admittedly, almost any maneuver can be made dangerous if a ship, contrary to reason and regulations, abruptly and at close range, turns across the bow of another.

(a) (2) Far from introducing a hazard, the fact that no speed margin was available should have emphasized, and indicated clearly to the HOBSON, the necessity of turning right and dropping back gradually, and not risking falling behind by some difficult and hazardous maneuver.

(a) (3) Possibly Captain McCaffree might well have stationed the HOBSON in her recovery station in advance of the turn, but this is not made mandatory by any tactical publication, nor is it always necessary or advisable. On a clear night, with the red truck lights, and with only three ships participating in a simple maneuver, the use of running lights is not considered to have been necessary.

(a) (4) No details are specified, and it is not known what Captain McCaffree, as OTC or as Commanding Officer, could have done under Article 27, International Rules of the Road, and under the circumstances existing, other than to perform the signaled maneuver properly, and when placed "in extremis" by the HOBSON to hold his course and to back with full power, all of which he did. He did have due regard for all dangers of collision.

(b) (1) Captain McCaffree did not "assume" the HOBSON had turned right initially, if by that carelessness is implied. He stated he felt such a turn the proper one, as did everyone else, including the two destroyer experts called by counsel for Lieutenant Commander Tierney, and in fact at the execution of the signal, "TURN 260° SPEED 27" the HOBSON did turn right at 130°T. There was no reason for him not to suppose that everything was proceeding normally in the execution of the signaled maneuver, until the HOBSON's final left turn.

(b) (2) At one minute prior to the collision the HOBSON was just starting her left turn, distant about 1250 yards from the WASP which ship was on course about 2510 [*sic* — *251°*] still coming right to the signaled course 260°. As can be seen from paragraph 9(b) following, Captain McCaffree and Lieutenant Herbst noted this turn quickly and promptly. True bearings and ranges, even if time had permitted their being taken, at this point would have done nothing but show the situation was one of "extremis," a fact already known. If taken earlier they would have shown a normal port-to-port passing condition. It is well to emphasize this point, a survey of the evidence, and an inspection of the tracks in the diagram submitted by the court as its opinion of the tracks of the two vessels, all show that prior to the HOBSON's left turn, bearings and ranges would have revealed nothing alarming. Only when the HOBSON made its left turn did the situation become dangerous. The evidence shows this turn was detected and the danger recognized promptly and as soon as could be expected.

(b) (3) The WASP actually changed exactly two, or two and one-half degrees, from her 260 degree course. Such change was not received by the HOBSON, could not have been detected by watching the WASP, and had the HOBSON detected it, would have had no effect on her evolution. True bearings and ranges of the HOBSON were not required by Captain McCaffree to decide when to adjust his course more nearly into the wind. It was obvious there was no danger until the HOBSON's left turn created it.

(b) (4) The first part of paragraph 18(b)(4) of the court's
opinion has been discussed in paragraph (a)(4) preceding, no further comment is necessary. With respect to the matter of "not keeping his course under
Article 21," the opinion of the court is not under-
stood. Prior to being placed "in extremis," the
WASP was adjusting its course to the left: she was
2° off the signaled course of 260° at the collision.
How this minute change, of which probably only
about 1 was made after WASP was "in extremis,"
could effect the HOBSON is not known. The matter of true compass bearings is discussed hereinafter in paragraph 9(a)(2) and will not be discussed here.

8. I disagree with paragraph 19 of the court's opinions because I
do not believe it states accurately the action of Captain McCaffree, and does not refer to responsibilities under Article 21,
International Rules of the Road.

The following opinion represents my view:

"That following the final left turn of the HOBSON,
which started less than one minute prior to the collision,
and considering the time required under darkened ship
conditions to determine this unexpected change of course,
Captain McCaffree took prompt and effective action, in
conformity with his responsibilities under Article 21 and
27, International Rules of the Road."

9. I disagree, in general, with paragraph 21 of the court's opinions
because:

(a) Negligence on the part of Lieutenant Herbst is not supported by any finding of fact, nor by the evidence.

There is no underline_causal connection_underline between the collision and any
of the so-called acts of negligence charged by the majority of
the court against Lieutenant Herbst, nor does the opinion of the
majority allege any such causal connection.

Specifically I disagree with paragraph 21 of the court's opinions in the following respects: (Note: For ease of reference the

following paragraphs carry the same numbers as the paragraphs of the court's opinions to which they refer.)

(a) Lieutenant Herbst, when asked if he thought that the HOBSON would turn right, replied that such was his expectation. The belief that the right turn was the proper evolution was supported by every witness, including the destroyer experts called by counsel for Lieutenant Commander Tierney. Thus, it is difficult to see how Lieutenant Herbst could have had any other expectation. (The HOBSON did turn right initially to 130°T.) Likewise, he was on very firm ground, and similarly supported, when he said he thought the HOBSON would slow down and fall back into position. To imply from this logical opinion any undue or improper relaxation of caution has no basis in evidence or fact.

(a) (1) Lieutenant Herbst testified he could see the HOBSON without the binoculars. He also stated he observed her through binoculars when she made her left turn. There is no evidence he could have detected her turn earlier by use of binoculars. Bearing on this point, Lieutenant Hoefer, OOD of the HOBSON, testified he could see the outline, hull, and flight deck of the WASP at 3800 yards without binoculars, and that he did not use binoculars during the maneuvers leading up to the collision.

(a) (2) Captain McCaffree was standing at the port pylorus [*pelorus — for taking relative bearings*] watching the HOBSON carefully, a fact known to Lieutenant Herbst and taken into account. Lieutenant Herbst himself observed the HOBSON but his duties as officer of the deck would not have permitted concentration on this ship alone. While not taking bearing with an alidade [*a straight-edge sighting apparatus*], Captain McCaffree was taking these by, as he expressed it, "seaman's eye," which meant that by combining the ship's heading and the relative bearing of the HOBSON he was in effect also getting true bearings. These bearings, call them relative or call them true, were sufficiently accurate to show the HOBSON's bearing changing to the left, and by freeing his eye from an alidade, permitted Captain McCaffree to give full attention to the situation. An exact true bearing would not have given him either course or range. Nor, considering the course open to the HOBSON to follow in taking her new position, and right loss of ranges or bearings, would he have been able to learn anything whatsoever not already known to him, namely, that the HOBSON was approaching, and if her course were continued, would pass him reasonably close aboard, at a range of about 500 yards. The statement that the HOBSON bore 350 degrees relative from the WASP, could be more accurately stated by saying that as the WASP passed through 251 degrees T while coming to her new heading, the HOBSON bore 350 degrees relative. There was no particular reason to know the exact course or range of the HOBSON so long as it did not threaten the WASP. There were many alternatives for the HOBSON to pursue in taking her new station, such as turning right with a small rudder angle, and slowing her speed by zig-zag plus a reduction in engine revolutions, or she could continue a course of 090 degrees T for an interval, then make her right turn. Thus she could have been on various courses and executed various movements without causing any alarm until she abruptly turned left when it was too late.

(b)   There is no evidence to support this view of the court, quite the contrary. The HOBSON's fatal left turn was ordered about 1"-10° before the collision and it would require about 30 seconds from that time to become noticeable. Until this turn was made the WASP was not "in extremis." Lieutenant Herbst gave uncontradicted testimony he observed the HOBSON through binoculars, noted her turn, and shouted, "Captain, we are in trouble." Immediately the Captain took action. There is no evidence that by any means he could have become aware earlier of the HOBSON's left turn. The essence of the matter is did Lieutenant Herbst detect the turn of the HOBSON as soon as could be expected? A time analysis will show this. Such an analysis has already partially been made, inasmuch as the position of the HOBSON at the time she gave the left order, and as shown on Diagram "X" of the court's opinions (approximate tracks of the WASP and HOBSON), was fixed by assuming it took 1"-0^s for the HOBSON to turn through 90°, at which point the collision occurred. Then a figure of 0"-10^s was added as representing the time between the giving of the order and the start of the turn, giving a total of 1"-10^s from time order was given for HOBSON's left turn to collision. The analysis continues:

(1) Time from start of turn to collision: 0"-60^s.

(2) Time from commencement of turn until it became perceptible: 0"-20^s.

   Note: Proved on data showing angle of turn of HOBSON.

(3) Time from moment WASP engine room commenced execution of order emergency astern until collision: 0"-30^s.

(4) Time left for Captain McCaffree to perceive, appraise, and transmit his order to engine room: 0"-10^s.

(5) Time remaining for Lieutenant Herbst to perceive, appraise, and shout his warning, "Captain, we are in trouble," slightly less than 0"-10^s, as he gave his warning before the Captain gave his order to engines: 0"-10^s(-).

   Conclusion: It is difficult to see how he or Captain McCaffree could have detected the HOBSON's turn any more quickly and acted any more promptly than they did.

(c) No details are specified, but nothing was required under Article 27 other than what was done. When the situation became one of "extremis," an order for the engines to back emergency speed was given, and the course was held. Had the WASP taken any other action it would have been in violation of the Article. The matter of compass bearings is covered in paragraph (a)(2) preceding.

10. I disagree with paragraph 23 of the opinions of the court because I believe the sole responsibility for the collision rests with Lieutenant Commander Tierney. My reasons for this belief have been set forth in detail elsewhere in my minority report on opinions, particularly in paragraphs 7 and 9 thereof. Nevertheless, my views are summarized here.

    (a)   The acts charged by the majority of the court against Captain McCaffree and Lieutenant Herbst in paragraphs 18 and 21 of the court's opinions, even were they substantiated, did not cause, and would not have prevented the collision. There was no causal connection, nor was any alleged.

    (b)   My views as to the non-substantiation of these so-called "acts of negligence" are given at length in my paragraphs 7 and 9 preceding. But even had any of them been substantiated, for the reasons indicated in (a) above, they would have constituted simply criticisms of Captain McCaffree's performance of duty as Officer in Tactical Command and Commanding Officer, and of Lieutenant Herbst as officer of the deck, the proper remedy for which, is appropriate action by their Type Commander.

My views as to the proper opinion here is: "That no person or persons, other than Lieutenant Commander Tierney, whose actions were the cause of the collision, are responsible for the collision."

RECOMMENDATIONS

1. I disagree with paragraph 1 of the court's recommendations because I believe Lieutenant Commander Tierney's dereliction of duty was the sole cause of the collision and that the word "direct" should be deleted.

2. [*This paragraph has been deleted in the released transcript.* — *B.P.*]

3. I disagree with paragraph 5a(1) of the court's recommendations because I think it is liable to misconstruction, and does not phrase accurately my views in this respect, specifically:

    (a) From it an inference might be drawn that a low state of training, and/or inexperience, of the two ships' companies as a whole, was a cause of the accident. Such was not the case. The fault lay with the judgment of competency of the Commanding Officer of the HOBSON. He was reasonably experienced, had been recommended for command of destroyers while serving as executive officer of one, and was considered competent and qualified by his division Commander. The Operational Commander in this case had every right to consider him competent and qualified.

    (b) The following is my recommendation as a substitute for that of the court: "That emphasis be placed by operating any type, including local type, commanders, on the state of training of units in scheduling and conduct of operations. That Operational and type Commanders take cognizance of the fact that, with an expanding Navy, the Commanding Officers and crews of ships are not automatically experienced and thoroughly competent, and that before advanced maneuvers are conducted, due consideration be given to the actual experience and state of training of the officers and crews. For example, when destroyers are detailed to plane guard duty, particularly duty involving operations at night with ships darkened, the officer detailing them should if any doubt exists in his mind as to their readiness, advise the prospective officer in tactical command of the operations, as to the state of training and readiness for such duty, of the destroyers so detailed."

                                           Osborne B. Hardison,
                                           Rear Admiral, U.S. Navy,
                                           President

The Pride of Indiana — The USS *Indianapolis*

HE FIRST Charles Butler McVay lived in Pittsburgh, Pennsylvania, where he headed the powerful Pittsburgh Trust Company. He was exceedingly proud of his son, Charles Butler McVay II, when he became a Midshipman at the U.S. Naval Academy in 1886. As an ardent supporter "out of uniform," and just when Annapolis was about to lose its identity due to budget cuts, McVay literally saved the school, and in expression of eternal gratitude he was made an honorary Midshipman on the occasion of his son's graduation in 1890. He wore his honorary class ring with pride.

Charles II proved that his father's trust and pride had been well founded. During his career, he served as a division officer on the USS *Amphitrite*, part of the U.S. Navy fleet that destroyed the Spanish ships in Santiago Harbor, Cuba, in 1898. He later commanded the cruiser USS *Saratoga*, the famous battleships USS *New Jersey* and USS *Oklahoma*, and the entire Asiatic fleet. McVay also served as the Washington Navy Yard Chief of the Bureau of Ordnance. He retired with the rank of Admiral in 1932.

Charles Butler McVay III, born at the turn of the 20th century, continued the family's long and glorious U.S. Navy tradition. Charles III followed his dad to Annapolis, where he was nicknamed "Cherub," no doubt because of his rosy cheeks and benign countenance. He graduated from the U.S. Naval Academy in 1920.

In early 1942, Charles McVay III was on shipboard duty in the Pacific. During the Solomon Islands campaign, while serving under Rear Admiral A. S. Merrill, he won the Silver Star when the Task Force sank two Japanese destroyers. In the April 1, 1945, attack on Okinawa, he earned a Bronze Star with V and a Purple Heart.

On November 18, 1944, his dream became reality when he took command of the recently repaired and refurbished cruiser USS *Indianapolis*.

The Washington Disarmament Treaty of 1922 had set the limitations of a flush-deck, rakish (trim, streamlined) cruiser at 10,000 tons. During the period 1929-1930, the United States had built two cruisers, the USS *Pensacola* (after the name of the class) and the *Salt Lake City*. In 1930 and 1931, a new class of six cruisers, 15 feet longer and several thousand tons heavier, had received the name of Northampton. In 1942, the Northampton Class USS *Houston* was lost in the Battle of the Java Sea. The *Northampton* and *Chicago* were lost in the Solomon Islands in 1943, and the remaining ships of the class, the *Chester*, *Louisville*, and *Augusta* were refitted to conform to modern standards.

The next USN cruiser class contained two ships, the *Portland* (for which the class is named) and the *Indianapolis*. Both were over 600 feet in length and displaced more than 13,000 tons. With the innovation of

The USS *Indianapolis* in wartime paint, with aircraft amidships.

"on-board" aircraft, it was necessary to find a place to put the aircraft support facilities. Thus, a gap had been opened amidships to allow for catapults and a hangar. The silhouette, which seemed somewhat incomplete, gave rise to the nickname of "Swayback Maru."

Though the *Indianapolis* had not the style of modern flush-deck cruisers, she had "class" that attracted Franklin Roosevelt. Shortly after taking office as President in 1933, Roosevelt had cruised the Atlantic, and again in 1935 he had reviewed the fleet from her bridge. He was on board her for the last time during his South American tour in 1936.

During the period of the Pacific unrest before America's entry into World War II, the *Indianapolis* had joined the fleet at Pearl Harbor. On the tragic morning of December 7, 1941, she had been engaged in gunnery practice off Johnston Island, more than 500 miles from the Japanese surprise attack. She had hurried to intercept the Japanese fleet but had been unable to find the enemy in her search area.

Thereupon, the *Indianapolis* was to avenge herself for being absent from the "day of infamy." During the Japanese resupply operations staged during the winter of 1942 and the spring of 1943, the cruiser stood off the Aleutians and, though not as brash as the old *Salt Lake City*, nevertheless managed to bag a Japanese ammunition ship. As the Japanese retreated from the Aleutian engagement, the U.S. Navy moved to the south.

During the island-hopping campaigns, the *Indianapolis* was there every time. In November 1943, she gave fire support at Tarawa, as the 2nd Marine Division stormed ashore at Betio on the southern tip of the atoll, and shot down a Japanese plane. The Marshall Islands were next, and she again bagged an aircraft in 1944.

In early 1945, in the Bonin Islands, some 500 miles south of Japan, the V Amphibious Corps' 4th and 5th Marine Divisions with three Marine divisions in reserve, attacked Iwo Jima; here again the cruiser bagged a Japanese plane.

In April of 1945, OPERATION ICEBERG, the invasion of Okinawa, began. The ground forces were under the Command of Lieutenant General Simon Bolivar Buckner, a departure from the screaming fury of Marine General Holland "Howling Mad" Smith. The hard-fought campaign for the island ended on June 21. For the first time, Japanese kamikaze aircraft became a factor; they inflicted their suicidal fury on large targets — the larger the better. The *Indianapolis* downed three of these planes before meeting the fourth, which dived into the ship, crashing onto the main deck but causing little damage. However, the plane's bomb had pierced the main deck and passed through the entire ship before exploding under the hull. Flooding was minimal, and, listing slightly, she was yet a manageable ship.

With Captain Charles McVay on the bridge, the *Indianapolis* returned to the Mare Island shipyard in San Francisco to correct the damage. The completion of repair coincided with an urgent need for a means to transport the uranium fuel of the first operational atomic bomb to the assembly station on the island of Tinian in the Mariana Islands. Though the weight of the fissionable material was slight — several hundred pounds, of minimal volume less than a cubic foot — it was not considered safe to transport such a critical cargo by plane, which might be shot down or lost. Similarly, a ship that could not protect itself from surface attack nor outrun any undersea attacker was unacceptable. The answer, then, was a fast Navy cruiser, and the one most available was the USS *Indianapolis*.

While the *Indianapolis* was concluding repair at the shipyard, a cloak-and-dagger operation was being conducted. An Army Major, Robert R. Furman, of the Corps of Engineers on the staff of the Manhattan Project, was chosen by Major General Leslie Groves (in charge of the atomic program) to watch over the uranium during its sea voyage and to deliver it intact to Tinian. Accompanying him was Captain James F. Nolan, the chief radiological officer of the Army Medical Corps. He was to "keep the monster under control." To give these two clandestine status, they were instructed to wear insignia of the Field Artillery. The two officers were so unfamiliar with service custom that they wore the crossed cannons upside down!

This bit of inconsequential trivia, however, could be explained away, because the officers were introverted and uninterested in uniforms or personal appearance, and the Navy hosts, unfamiliar with Army insignia, cared little which way their insignia were worn. In the U.S. Navy, as long as an officer wore two of every type of insignia — two identical collar insignia, except mirrored Captain's eagles, and two shoulder boards —

there was no way that they could be worn upside down. (It is interesting to note that the U.S. Public Health Service is an exception, for its shoulder boards have mirrored insignia, which must be worn with the anchor flukes pointed forward, if one is not to be accused of dragging anchor.)

Major Furman had first met Robert Oppenheimer, director of the atomic bomb development, in Santa Fe, New Mexico, then had journeyed to Los Alamos where he was introduced to Captain Nolan. Though each knew something of what he was to do, neither would discuss the assignment in detail nor postulate on the outcome.

On Friday, July 13, 1945, an Army "Jimmy" (GMC 2½-ton truck) painted black and fitted with an ordnance-type closed metal body, was loaded with the one canister — a cylinder 1½ feet in diameter and 2 feet in length. Furman and Nolan rode in an automobile behind the truck. After the slight misadventure of a flat tire, they arrived at Kirtland Field in Albuquerque where three DC-3s were waiting to carry the convoy to Hamilton Field near San Francisco. From there the canister was sent to Hunters Point, San Francisco, to meet the *Indianapolis*.

The loading of the uranium was carried out in the early morning hours and was not unlike an execution, what with all the secrecy and formality. At 0300, on the morning of July 16, the crew was awakened with the word that preparations to get under way were to be made immediately and that a work detail was to report on the hangar deck. Captain McVay told the sleepy officers that a secret cargo would soon arrive, and once it was stowed, the ship would cast off for Tinian.

At 1400, the three Army trucks arrived and positioned themselves alongside the ship. Gently a wheel-mounted gantry crane hoisted the small canister aboard and placed it on the hangar deck. Under the ever-watchful eyes of the Marine guards, the canister was secured to the deck by metal straps welded down and finally affixed with a padlock, the key of which was in the pocket of Major Furman. (It is not known whether or not Captain McVay and/or someone aboard knew what was being transported, but the scuttlebutt was that the canister contained spores from some dreaded disease, which the United States was to inflict upon Japan in order to shorten the war and obviate the need for an invasion.)

At 0836 Pacific Standard Time, the USS *Indianapolis* sailed under San Francisco's Golden Gate Bridge outward bound. Once the Farallon Islands had been passed, some 26 miles from the Golden Gate, McVay put the ship to 29 knots, and by nightfall she was nearing her flank speed of 30 knots. She slacked off top speed several times during the record passage to Honolulu.

During the run, the ship's gunnery officer, Commander Stanley Lipski, invited the two Army "Artillery" officers to witness naval gunnery practice and to critique the performance. Nolan, an M.D., feigned seasickness and declined, but Furman made an appearance and put on a good show, though he knew nothing of artillery behavior.

Some excitement occurred when a minor fire broke out after suitcases and handbags stacked too close to the forward funnel began to smolder. A fire party quickly put the blaze out, but ruined baggage was the result.

The third night out offered additional excitement when radar man Harold Schecterle's appendix was removed under local anesthetic in the sickbay.

The next morning the sight of Diamond Head signaled arrival in Hawaii — 3,000 miles in 75 hours — a new record. Special treatment was bestowed upon the USS *Indianapolis* by the battleships in Honolulu, but no one knew why — after all, she was just another cruiser.

At Pearl Harbor all passengers for Hawaii were debarked, but not the crew, who were destined to remain aboard. Upon departure from Honolulu for Tinian at 1500, the only outlanders aboard were Major Furman and Captain Nolan and their strange "genie in a bottle," waiting, like the contents of Pandora's Box, to be set free.

Because the ship was ahead of schedule, Captain McVay was advised to slacken speed, which he did, to 24 knots, which he maintained, for the remainder of the voyage.

When the Navy Forward Area was reached, about halfway to Tinian, the fleet operating instructions limited the speed of ships to 16 knots, unless there was dire reason to exceed this. The reduced speed negated the advantage that a fast ship — a cruiser — had over a submarine, and presented the question, "Should the *Indianapolis* be given an escort?" The reason for the speed limitation was to conserve fuel, and the reason an escort was declined was that no submarine would waste a torpedo on a vessel it knew to be too fast to overtake.

On July 16, 1945, the same day that the USS *Indianapolis* departed San Francisco, the Japanese submarine I-*58,* commanded by Lieutenant Commander Mochitsura Hashimoto, set sail. The two antagonists were to meet in two weeks.

Commander Hashimoto had been born in the ancient capital city of Kyoto in 1909. His father, a Shinto priest in a fairly important shrine, could ill afford to put funds to the task of assuring his son an appointment to the naval academy, but Mochitsura had managed to enter the academy in 1927, the year that he had graduated from high school. He was one of nine children; his oldest brother, a graduate of the military academy, was on duty with the army. Mochitsura graduated from the naval academy in 1931, at which time Japan was engaged in establishing Manchuria as a puppet state.

Hashimoto had been assigned to submarines in 1934. Three years later he was to get his first taste of the real war; his oldest brother, then a full Colonel, was killed in Manchuria. That same year, Hashimoto married the daughter of a well-to-do businessman. He was assigned to the submarine school in 1938 and torpedo school in 1939. At age 39, in 1941, he looked forward to a bright career in the submarine service, and like most thinking people in Japan, believed that the immediate future would mean war with America.

At the time of Pearl Harbor, Hashimoto was assigned to the submarine I-*24* as a torpedo officer. In mid-November 1941, with a midget submarine bolted to her deck, I-*24* joined three other submarines, similarly outfitted, and set sail for a rendezvous off Pearl Harbor. On Saturday night, December 6, the sub surfaced off Waikiki and listened for a time to American dance music. Excitedly, they went below and lay there until morning when they surfaced and launched Lieutenant Kazou Sakamaki with crewman Kyoji Inagaki in a midget submarine. Their midget hung up on a reef, and Inagaki was never found. But Lieutenant Sakamaki was captured, acquiring the dubious honor of being the first prisoner of the Americans in World War II. Hashimoto subsequently returned to Japan, and commanded the

RO-*31*, RO-*44*, and I-*158* in home waters. In May 1944, he took command of I-*58*.

To the credit of the USS *Indianapolis*, she was sunk by the best Japan had to offer, better even than the best submarines that the United States had at the time. The I-*58* was nearly 360 feet long, with a beam of 30 feet, and displaced 2,150 tons. Larger than German or American submarines, she was powered by two diesels linked to batteries which, together, gave her an underwater cruising speed of 3 knots and a surface speed of 14 knots. She carried 19 of the Type 95 oxygen-fueled and wakeless torpedoes, which could be fired from any of six forward tubes. The torpedoes could achieve the unbelievable speed underwater of more than 45 knots and could strike a target nearly 10,000 yards away — 5½ miles! The 2-foot diameter torpedoes were armed with magnetic- or inertia-firing devices and carried 1,200 pounds of TNT. The I-*58* was equipped with surface and underwater radar and both electronic and acoustic sonar. Much of the normal deck and cabin equipment had been removed to make room for the six manned suicide kaiten torpedoes — the Japanese navy counterparts to the kamikaze.

The kaiten pilots were not of the submarine's regular crew but were a special branch of the service. They came two to a vessel, though the kaiten required but one crewman. Neither kaiten nor crewman ever returned. The redundancy in crew is evidence that Japan thought the kaiten and the kamikaze, together, would turn the tide of the war — much as Germany's Führer, Adolf Hitler, had thought that buzz bombs would make England kneel and phantom armies would rescue Berlin.

At the time of her commissioning in September of 1944, the Japanese I-*58* submarine carried a total crew of 105 officers and men — five Lieutenants for the various divisions and one Lieutenant Junior Grade as gunnery officer. It was obvious who would be the officer of choice to rid the ship of rats, which came aboard before the last welder left. Being the *only* junior officer does not bode well for one's health.

The I-*58*'s first cruise was to Guam to attack the American invaders. In the early morning of January 12, 1945, she dispatched four kaitens. Hearing some muffled explosions, those aboard chose to claim a tanker, though no official inquiry has confirmed the claim. This done, the submarine hightailed it back to the base at Kure, Japan.

For the next several months the I-58 was in and out of port, until she finally, in April, was ordered to help defend Okinawa. Try that she might, she gave no account of herself save that on April 29 she was the only submarine to return from Okinawa. There she waited in her home port, until that fateful day, July 15, when she quit Kure under orders to "harass enemy communications." Lieutenant Commander Hashimoto's first destination was to try the Mariana Islands-Okinawa route, and when this proved unsuccessful, the intersection of the Guam-Leyte and the Okinawa-Palau routes was selected as the most likely place to find Allied shipping.

Meanwhile, the orders for the USS *Indianapolis*, once the uranium was safe ashore, were to proceed to Guam and thence to Leyte on the west coast of the Philippines. On leaving Tinian she came under the control of CINCPAC (Commander in Chief Pacific) Admiral Chester E. Nimitz. Her assignment was to engage in two weeks of training before becoming a part of Task Force 95, which was commanded by Vice Admiral J. B. Oldendorf, and Task Group 95.7, which was commanded by Rear Admiral L. D. McCormick. The orders were dispatched but garbled when received by TG 95.7, which never requested a repeat, and merely filed them with the briefest note by TG 95.

The vessel arrived in Agana, Guam, on July 25. Captain McVay met that day with CINCPAC Chief of Staff Commodore J. B. Carter and lunched with Admiral Raymond Spruance. The latter, planning for a role in the invasion armada of Japan, had selected the *Indianapolis* as his flagship. Spruance would have her wait for him in the Philippines until needed as his Command ship.

When Captain McVay checked with the routing officer, he was told that the speed limitation was yet in effect and that an escort was not available, nor was this necessary, for the line beyond which a ship could not travel without an escort was now well north of Guam. McVay was clearly led to believe that the danger of a submarine attack was minimal and that, should one be detected, the ship could outrun the submarine, for the disparity between the speed of the cruiser at 16 knots and a submarine at 5 knots needed no mathematical analysis.

The distance between Agana and Leyte was 1,165 nautical miles, and at the authorized speed of 15.8 knots and departure at 0900 on July 28, 1945, the cruiser was expected to arrive in Leyte at noon on July 31. At his discretion per orders, Captain McVay was to decide whether to "zig-zag" or not. On clearing the harbor, the Port Director sent a dispatch to CTG 95.7 [*Commander Task Group*] with information to CTG 95 that the *Indianapolis* had departed Guam and had an estimated time of arrival to Leyte Gulf at 1100 on July 31st.

At noon Sunday, July 29, the day after departure, the ship hailed an LST going north and they passed a high sign. The LST was the last American ship to have made contact with the *Indianapolis* until her garbled message went out after she had been torpedoed.

A message was received by the *Indianapolis* in mid-afternoon on the 29th saying that a periscope had been sighted at 10 degrees, 25 minutes North, 131 degrees, 45 minutes East, some 70 miles south of the position that she would reach at midnight. Interestingly, in the wardroom that evening at the meal, there was jocular patter about the sub they were to "run over" that night. The ship had been zigzagging all day, but at dusk Captain McVay had ordered this ceased. Like the proud lady she was, the *Indianapolis* would be cleaving a straight path on her last night alive. Visibility was poor due to cloud cover, which broke only occasionally to reveal the moon, but as the night wore on, visibility improved and a waning moon shone through.

As usual, the sailors, with blankets and pillows, crowded the open deck in order to sleep in comfort. An errant light was observed coming from a porthole, and when traced down, was identified as coming from the space occupied by the "flyboys." The opening was secured, but no report was made of the violation.

Later, in the Court of Inquiry, there was much testimony about the deficiencies of the openness of the interior spaces on the main deck — there were no bulkheads separating areas. Perhaps this was poor design, but it is hardly likely that had the ship been built with bulkheads throughout, she would have survived after the torpedo strike, for the damage done was far below the main deck.

Just after midnight a torpedo struck the forward part of the ship, followed soon by another farther aft, about midship. The blasts took out all the ship's communication systems. Now orders had to be transmitted by messenger, or by shouting, and word of their plight could only be sent by emergency transmitter. Captain McVay, who had hastened to the bridge, had sent runners to assess the damage. They returned with dire reports. The forward compartments were filling so fast that the bow would soon disappear. The *Indianapolis* WAS SINKING! A slight list to starboard was noticed.

Captain McVay's greatest worry was whether a message had been sent, *and received*, giving the ship's plight and its location. But there was not time to loiter while the message could be transmitted again and again until someone acknowledged. McVay then issued the most painful order of his life: "Abandon ship!" With such an order all organizational structure came to an end; shipboard drill became reality. There are no contingency plans at this moment, for survival at sea must maximize the need to respond to any of a thousand possibilities — none of them pleasant.

The cruiser's condition and the plight of her crew were ominous. She was more than 300 nautical miles from the nearest land; there had not been one dispatch sent from the ship since she had left Guam, and none received. She was not expected for another 36 hours, and even then, her late arrival would not be shifted to distress and search for another 24 hours. They must wait 60 hours until someone finally realized they were in trouble, had been sunk or something else dire, and then and only then would the U.S. Navy begin to look for them.

As it turned out, the floating survivors of the *Indianapolis* were found only as a result of a chance sighting by a routine patrol.

On July 27, 1945, the Japanese submarine I-*58* had arrived on the Guam-Leyte route. The next day, after submerging in order to escape detection by a Catalina PBY flying boat scouting the area, she rose to periscope depth again and found a tanker escorted by a destroyer. Lieutenant Commander Hashimoto, fearing that there would not be another chance to strike at the enemy, launched two kaitens — one piloted by a Lieutenant Ban, and the other by an enlisted pilot named Komori. Long agonizing moments preceded an explosion, which meant the tanker had been struck, or a kaiten had gone aground — or had been spotted and sunk. Bad weather prevented the submarine from surfacing and finding out. The Commander reported, "Tanker sunk," but it was believed to be an optimistic conclusion to the fragmentary information available.

All day Sunday, the 29th, the I-58 had cruised the juncture with no luck. At nearly midnight the submarine rose once more to periscope depth and began to look around. At a distance of nearly seven miles and silhouetted against the moon was a black object, which the excited Commander judged to be a battleship or a cruiser. Hashimoto positioned the sub and began preparing for a torpedo attack. When the intended target — the USS *Indianapolis* — had come within the distance of 2½ miles, the I-58 had to maneuver to avoid being rundown by the cruiser. Hashimoto planned to fire at the distance of 1¼ miles but at the last minute waited until the target had closed to a mile away.

Then Hashimoto gave the order to fire six torpedoes. Columns of water rose alongside the forward turret of the cruiser, followed by a bright orange flame. Repeated explosions occurred on the target. Hashimoto let those in the conn see what had been done and then, fearing depth charges, he submerged. Believing that the *Indianapolis* might not be sinking and that she might have underwater detection aboard, Hashimoto reloaded and returned to periscope depth to see what damage had been done. Surprisingly he found nothing — no debris nor flotsam. Seeking some proof of the sinking, he surfaced, but not within the area where survivors were struggling with the reality of having been torpedoed.

Several hours of fruitless search led to the departure of I-58 at 0300, yet on the surface. At this time, Hashimoto dispatched to the Sixth Fleet in Kure and the Combined Fleets in Sagamihara the message — erroneous — that he had torpedoed and sunk a "battleship of the Idaho Class." The message was sent by a simple code and on a frequency normally used by the Japanese navy. During the heat of warfare, the U.S. Navy would have been monitoring every word transmitted on the frequency; but now, with the flush of anticipated victory all but realized, the monitoring stations were not being manned, and the first word of a sinking, given by the

Commander Mochitsura Hashimoto at the periscope of the Japanese submarine I-*58*.

Japanese, was not even heard by those who were supposedly responsible for the ship.

The I-*58* had sunk the cruiser *Indianapolis* shortly after midnight on July 30, 1945. She was the last major ship lost during World War II. A few days later, as the submarine crew steamed northward, they were monitoring American broadcasts of an important ship having been lost. By then, survivors had been seen and were being rescued. After Hashimoto's sinking of the cruiser had been learned by the Imperial Command, and before his actual return to Japanese soil, it had been judged fitting to promote him to full Commander.

On August 7, 1945, American radio reported that an "atomic bomb" had destroyed Hiroshima, Japan; the Nagasaki bomb followed on August 9. Still at sea, I-*58*'s crew was not panic-stricken because they had seen much of the war on land and at sea, and they could not quite comprehend the terrible consequences of such a bomb.

On August 10th, the I-*58* sighted a convoy; kaitens were launched and destroyed a tanker. On the 12th, another convoy, another launch of kaitens, and a merchant ship as a prize. On the 15th, the sub entered Bungo Strait, off of Japan's southernmost island of Kyushu, to return to her base. The crews had achieved great victories on their cruise, and they were happy to have returned safely. That evening, August 15, 1945, they received word that Japan had surrendered. Hashimoto praised the crew for their valiant effort, though he still did not know that it was the *Indianapolis* that they had sunk. The I-*58* was captured at her dock by the Americans, who kept her for eight months and then took her to sea and sunk her with explosives.

Was she the last Samurai?

The United States Navy positioned the USS *Indianapolis*'s sinking at 134 degrees, 48 minutes East, and 12 degrees, 2 minutes North. Hashimoto had a slightly different position: 134 degrees, 16 minutes East, and 12 degrees, 31 minutes North. At the time the attack began, the cruiser had 1,196 officers and men at muster. In the 12 minutes between the first torpedo strike and the sinking, those who were able abandoned the ship. It is not believed that any remained aboard to be trapped alive when she sank. Because no radio message had been received, no one knew either of her sinking or of the plight of her crew who were now swimming in the Philippine Sea. None of her boats had been launched, and many of the rafts that made it into the water had either lost their provisions or the goods were waterlogged. Most all of the survivors were wearing life jackets. The seas were calm.

The Navy life jacket was a vest, secured by drawstring and filled with kapok. Tests had shown that the vest would retain positive buoyancy for a period of at least 48 hours. Had not the seamen been told many times in survival training that a person in the sea could reasonably expect to be rescued within 24 hours?

Those who had been wounded during the torpedo attack and those who had been burned horribly were the first to die. Some of the men on rafts hailed other rafts to join with them, and lashed together to pool numbers, share provisions, and present a greater visibility to rescuers. At the time of the sinking there had been a mild, ten-knot wind from the southwest, while the current moved west and south. Those on the rafts were blown by the wind and those in the water moved only with the current, and they became separated. The dead were divested of their life jackets, which were given to sailors without them. The sailors were covered with oil. Inhalation and swallowing the oil scum on the

The USS *Indianapolis* survivors found on rafts.

surface had produced vomiting, smarting of eyes, breathing discomfort, and general distress.

Seaman Schecterle, the recipient of the appendectomy, used both his life jacket and a lard can to keep afloat. Small groups of the crew began to become isolated from each other. Later, after rescue, when they would tell of the ordeal, it was each time repeated that their lives became dependent on those in their small group who were yet alive. They thought of each other and rescue. Daylight allowed several of the groups to lash together and become a part of a larger unit.

On Monday, July 30th, the survivors saw a number of planes overhead, but the aircrew did not notice the men in the water. However, just the sight of the planes gave the men hope that a rescue might soon follow.

Sharks appeared and made off with one seaman. Near panic ensued, but as the attacks abated, calm returned to the stricken group. Monday was also a day of promise, for it was known that on that day the USS *Indianapolis* was to have fired at towed targets. Certainly when the tow planes arrived at the appointed rendezvous, and no ship was found, the disappearance would be flashed throughout the sector and activate an intense search. The men welcomed the coming of night, for it brought an end to the brutal sun. But after a few hours of the dark loneliness, the survivors longed for a return of daylight.

On Tuesday, July 31st, the wind stopped, the sea moderated, and external forces abated. It was a good omen! But the sun was ever present, burning exposed body parts and dehydrating the men's systems. Several of the survivors, though cautioned not to do so, drank seawater and paid for their mistake by death. The following day passed as before, and the night was a repetition of the previous one.

On Wednesday, August 1st, the survivors began bickering for position on the rafts, for possession of a lifebelt, for the meager food, and for past actions, which might in some way be responsible for the discomfort that was now being felt. The first instances of delirium were seen as some began to hallucinate — perhaps the result of exhaustion or the effects of the ingestion of seawater. Whatever, the manifestations were bizarre. Some men saw Japanese soldiers on their raft, others saw comrades who had perished in the sinking or later in the water. The number of those who died during that day rose to exceed the number who had succumbed during the night and on the day following the sinking. Clearly the plight of the survivors was critical. Their life jackets had become waterlogged — they would not serve much longer to keep the men afloat.

On Thursday, August 2nd, in the late afternoon, a Navy airplane passed overhead, but flew on despite the arm-waving and shouting of the men in the water. Curses followed as the plane and their hopes flew away. Then a strange and wonderful thing happened. The plane banked and, having made a tight circle, flew over them at a lower altitude. They knew that they were saved! It had been nearly 85 hours since they had been torpedoed.

The aircrew threw life jackets and rafts to the clusters of men. A second airplane joined the one circling, but its aircrew realized that all that could be done was to drop survival gear and to send out radio calls for help. By then, the survivors thought that only a vessel could actually pick them up.

But, as if too good to be true, a big, ugly, lumbering PBY flew in low to land, despite the swells, taxiing over to cluster after cluster. With the help of its crew, the survivors were guided or carried to rafts. After dark, a second PBY landed and joined in the patrolling, group to group, helping or taking aboard those too weak to remain longer in the water.

Captain McVay's group had drifted miles to the north and could only watch the rescue operations from afar, but with some assurance that their time would come eventually. Then in the dark, they saw a light become stronger. At ten in the evening a ship came upon these last of the survivors. The men were rescued — more than 100 hours after their ship's sinking.

The USS *Cecil J. Doyle*, a destroyer escort (DE), was the first of the rescue vessels to reach the survivors. She began the immediate task of combing the area and picking up those that were found. But she needed help and she did not know if other ships had been given the rescue mission and would arrive soon. The question, which troubled Commander Graham Clayton, was how to signal the urgency without disclosing to the Japanese that they had sunk an American cruiser. He made two Command decisions. Clayton turned on the ship's lights to aid the rescue and radioed on an open frequency that survivors of the *Indianapolis* had been found and requested assistance.

The destroyer escort's whaleboat was put to transferring survivors from the PBYs to the destroyer. By dawn nearly a hundred men had been brought aboard to the *Doyle* or found and picked up by her. One of the PBYs had served its purpose, but had been too damaged in landing on the water to attempt a takeoff and was sunk by the ship's gunfire.

The USS *Bassett*, a destroyer converted to a high-speed transport in 1944, arrived from the west and assisted the *Doyle* in the rescue. The *Talbot*, *Madison*, *Ringness*, and *Register* soon joined, and all found scattered survivors whom they fished from the water. The *Bassett*, a ship from the force that was derisively called "MacArthur's Navy" — part of the Seventh Amphibious Force assigned to retake the Philippines — sped away from the scene, bound for Samar Island in the Philippines, after having rescued 200 seamen. All the other rescue ships steamed south to Peleliu with their survivors. The hospital ship *Tranquility* picked up crew

Captain Charles B. McVay III and his wife at the U.S. Court of Inquiry.

members, including Captain McVay in Guam, and transferred them to Peleliu. The rescue had ended. The ships that remained at the scene spent their time collecting the dead as well as equipment for evidence of the tragedy. Out of a crew of 1,196 men, 900 had made it into the water, but only 316 were still alive after five days.

During those hectic days, Russia had entered the war on August 8th, the atomic bombs had been dropped successively on Hiroshima and Nagasaki on August 6th and 9th, and word had come that Japan was willing to talk of peace.

Scarcely had the discovery of the floating survivors of the *Indianapolis* been flashed to the Navy echelons than the covering of flanks began. Various Commands went to great length to cite the following of established protocols, and within scant weeks it had been firmly fixed that the culprit was not to be found within one of the shore-bound Commands but on the ship, in the form of Captain Charles B. McVay III. Even as the time-honored Court of Inquiry was being convened, there was a pervading sentiment to fix the blame on McVay, but not deal with him too harshly.

The U.S. Navy, at the height of the exuberance of the ending of the war, had announced the sinking. It was possible — just possible — that the announcement was timed with the euphoria so that the significance of the sinking of a cruiser and the subsequent seeming indifference to her whereabouts would not be such a blow to the American people. But voices raised questions that the Navy would not come to answer.

Admiral Nimitz appointed the Court of Inquiry comprised of Vice Admiral Charles A. Lockwood, Jr., Submarine Commander in the Pacific; Admiral George D. Murray, Mariana Islands Commander; and Rear Admiral Francis Whit-

Commander Mochitsura Hashimoto en route to the United States to testify at the Court of Inquiry into the sinking of the USS *Indianapolis*.

ing. The court convened on the morning of August 13, 1945, at the Navy base on Guam. No one, as yet, had hit upon the "up-stage" idea of finding and "hiring" the I-*58* Commander Hashimoto. In reality, until the initial days of the Court of Inquiry, no one really knew if the cruiser had struck a mine or had been torpedoed. Once it had been generally established that she had probably been torpedoed, the question of culpability of her Captain followed, and to protect McVay's rights, he was named an "interested party" and thus entitled to attend all proceedings (meetings) and, as well, to have present counsel of his choosing.

The inquiry came at a time when no one welcomed it as a diversion — the war was over and no one wanted to have anything to do with dragging a "red herring" across the road. But congressmen, representing irate parents who had lost sailors in the sinking, were intent on having "heads roll."

The court had as its main concern the operational failure that had allowed the vessel to go "unaccounted for" over *four days*! The court heard more than 40 witnesses, and in the end a decision had to be reached.

While yet in deliberation, President Harry S. Truman announced peace with Japan on August 15th. Almost simultaneously came the press release, which read, "The USS *Indianapolis* has been lost as a result of enemy action." There would be some dichotomy in the ending of the war and immediately thereafter being notified of the loss of a son, or husband, or father — clearly this all could not have come at a worse time. Furthermore, the cruiser had not fired even one shot in retaliation. The frustration could be quantified, with only the 316 rescued out of 1,196. It has been estimated that the torpedo accounted for approximately 300 deaths, and the remainder perished because the U.S. Navy was asleep.

The court completed its inquiry and deliberations, and on August 20 issued letters of reprimand to Captain McVay and Lieutenant Gibson and a letter of admonition to Lieutenant Commander Sancho. Gibson was the port officer who should have been alert to the non-arrival of the ship. He said that he had been complying fully with orders and Standard Operating Procedure.

Over three months later, the Navy sent a shot screaming across the bow when on November 27th it announced that Captain McVay would be court-martialed. The press greeted this decision to blame McVay alone as making him the scapegoat, to cover the U.S. Navy's indifference to the whereabouts of a cruiser for *four days*!

Captain McVay's court-martial began on December 3, 1945, at the Washington Navy Yard. The conspirators in the assassination of President Abraham Lincoln had been hanged at the same location! Was public sentiment again demanding the rolling of a head? If so, this "head-rolling" would be seen, for it had been ordered that the trial would be held in public, as "dirty linen."

John P. Cady, Captain USN, who had known McVay at the Naval Academy as an underclassman, represented him. Cady had a law degree from George Washington University. His opponent, as Judge Advocate, was Medal of Honor and Navy Cross holder, Captain Thomas Ryan.

In court-martial procedure, the Charge, and Specification of Charge (the latter being an amplification), against Captain McVay were as stated below:

CHARGE I
Through Negligence Suffering a Vessel of the Navy to be Hazarded.

SPECIFICATION
In that Charles B. McVay, III, Captain, U.S. Navy, while so serving in command of the U.S.S. *Indianapolis*, making passage singly, without escort, from Guam, Mariana's [*sic*] Islands, to Leyte, Philippine Islands, through an area in which enemy submarines might be encountered, did, during good visibility after moonrise on 29 July 1945, at or about 10:50 p.m. minus nine and one-half zone time, neglect and fail to exercise proper care and attention to the safety of said vessel in that he neglected and failed, then and thereafter, to cause a zigzag course to be steered, and he, the said McVay, through said negligence, did suffer the said U.S.S. *Indianapolis* to be hazarded, the United States then being in a state of war.

CHARGE II
Culpable Inefficiency in the Performance of Duty.

SPECIFICATION
In that Charles B. McVay, III, Captain, U.S. Navy, while so serving in command of the U.S.S. *Indianapolis*, making passage from Guam, Marianas, to Leyte, Philippine Islands, having been informed at or about 12:10 a.m., minus nine and one-half zone time, on 30 July 1945, that said vessel was badly damaged

and in sinking condition, did then and there fail to issue and see effected such timely orders as were necessary to cause said vessel to be abandoned, as it was his duty to do, by reason of which inefficiency many persons on board perished with the sinking of said vessel, the United States then being in a state of war.

/s/ James Forrestal.
[*Secretary of the Navy*]

At the beginning of the trial Captain McVay replied to the charges with the statement, "Not guilty." Lieutenant Waldren, the routing officer from Guam, who had been summoned to Washington to testify, recounted the details of the departure of the ship and, on examination, acknowledged that McVay had requested an escort. As none was available, and as a cruiser could outrun any submarine afloat, the request had been declined. Lieutenant Waldren was questioned about the route that the ship had followed to its doom. He replied that it was the most direct and had been chosen by McVay and approved "upstairs," because it was believed that there was no danger.

Waldren's testimony was contradicted by the next witness for the service, Lieutenant Commander Alan McFarland, a destroyer Commander who, as one who had sailed frequently along the course followed by McVay, was presented as an "expert" in proper voyage procedures, *i.e.*, speed, whether to follow a straight course or to zigzag, or whether to follow restrictive procedures mandated elsewhere in more hostile waters. When asked if he would have followed more cautious procedures, he replied "yes," but his reply was challenged, and the challenge sustained, for it was affirmed that McFarland was "not an experienced cruiser Commander."

Because enemy submarines had been reported in the area, McFarland was asked if these sightings could have placed the sighted subs at the scene of the sinking at the correct time, and the reply was affirmative. However, this thesis was later made moot when it was established that Hashimoto's submarine was not one of those sighted but rather an unsighted, unplotted enemy submarine.

An astronomer testified as to the weather and conditions of visibility in intermittent moonlight at the time and place of the attack.

An officer of the staff of the Secretary of the Navy cited a letter from Captain McVay to Secretary James V. Forrestal reporting on the sinking, in which he described the conditions as "intermittent moonlight and unlimited visibility." McVay strongly protested the misunderstanding of this statement. He claimed the statement was "routine" and that he was under stress when the letter was written. In fact, it was so dark on the bridge that he couldn't see his hand before his face. He was unable to explain why he had not changed this statement, if he now testified that it was incorrect. He replied that he had thought no more about the matter, since he had not believed, until this very moment, that his words would be used to establish a condition of visibility and speed, which would have required his cruiser to zigzag.

Next to testify were some of the survivors whose knowledge of the event were considered relevant and of benefit to the prosecution. Lieutenant McKissick, deck officer during twilight, stated that the visibility had been intermittent (poor) and that zigzagging would have been followed by him (by his order) had it not been so, and had it been ordered, he was sure McVay would have approved. He said that there had been reports on the bridge of Japanese submarines 200 miles ahead and 200 miles south, but none reported in the vicinity that the cruiser would have cleared before the sun rose. He said that he believed the order to abandon ship had been timely and that probably 900 men had jumped safely into the water; the remainder were either trapped below or were dead or so disabled to have been rendered helpless.

Lieutenant Redmayne, assistant to the actual deck officer, Commander Lipski, testified next. Lipski had died in abandoning ship, and it was up to his assistant to tell what had happened. Redmayne stated that the visibility had been poor until about 2300, when the moon had appeared intermittently through the clouds. He acknowledged that the ship had not been zigzagging and testified that he did not believe it had been necessary to do so. Redmayne's estimate of 800 crewmen who made it safely into the water was a bit lower than that of McKissick.

WHAT HAPPENED ONCE THEY WERE IN THE WATER, AND HOW LONG THEY HAD TO WAIT WAS NOT IN THE PURVIEW OF THE COURT. But this was also a two-edged sword, for Captain McVay had taken the position that he could not be held responsible for what occurred AFTER the sinking since he had no control over these events. Perhaps it would have been better strategy had the defense included all events, since it was the inappropriate loss of life that had caused the court-martial to be convened; had there not been great loss and had rescue been prompt, the earlier Court of Inquiry would have been sufficient to take away a few files of advancement — McVay's position on the promotion list reduced — but no more.

The ship's bugler, David Mack, testified that he had stood around during the hours before being torpedoed waiting to play several of the routine calls — tattoo and taps. He had been holding his bugle when the torpedo hit, and he had been ready to play "abandon ship" should he have been given the order to do so. He readily admitted that he doubted that many of the men on board would have known the call had they heard it. He could not remember where he was or if he had his bugle in hand when the actual order was given to abandon ship.

Ensign Woolson, the Damage Control Officer, had been at sea for two weeks total before the tragedy. He said that the forward torpedo hit had killed most of the crew in the fo'c's'le (forecastle) and that the aft torpedo had silenced the ship's communications. Woolson testified that the ship had been in reasonably good condition to be traveling at sea, and had not been endangered; there were no restrictions that would have hindered the safety or abandonment of the ship. Neither of the two motor whaleboats had been launched, but 12 of 36 rafts and 6 of 25 floater nets had been dropped. Woolson had been a good witness — articulate, poised, and in command of what he had to say.

A radioman named Moran testified that he was the only survivor of the communications staff. A message had been received on Sunday about a merchant ship having been torpedoed some 200 miles south of their position at the time of the sinking. He had stayed in the communications shack attempting to send a message until the ship's list was so great as to cause the radio equipment to topple off its tables. It was only then that they went out to abandon ship. He also said that none of their messages had been electrically powered since the torpedo hit and that they were attempting to rouse power from alternate sources.

Ensign Rogers set the time of torpedoing at 0010, which would have put the ship in only one hour of good visibility before the torpedoing. Had Hashimoto happened along one hour earlier, he probably would not have seen the USS *Indianapolis*.

A supply officer, Lieutenant Reid, testified that he had been on the fantail (stern) during the congregation of sailors who were moving upward along the listing deck, and from which location he had witnessed their departure from the ship before he abandoned. Other witnesses corroborated the previous testimony.

The auspicious beginning of the trial was to be shaken somewhat the very next week when the trial resumed with the appearance of Commander Hashimoto. He had been found in Japan after his submarine had been identified as the one that had sunk the *Indianapolis*, and had been brought to the United States to shed all possible light on the grisly tragedy.

Of course, Hashimoto did not seek to appear at the trial, but was ordered to do so by his American captors. He came escorted by an American officer and was ensconced in quarters at the Washington Navy Yard under constant guard. His arrival was a bombshell to America and an insult to many. Robert Roark, the noted columnist, wrote that it was unnecessary and done only to bolster the publicity of a sagging court-martial by a publicity-seeking Navy. The *Washington Post* accused the Navy of putting a vanquished enemy in the position of being judge of the actions of an officer of the country who had just defeated Japan. The representatives of several veterans organizations spoke in bitter opposition.

It must be remembered that at the end of World War II a move was underfoot to redefine the mission of the armed services. The U.S. Air Force was to become a separate service in 1947, and there was talk of the need to abolish the U.S. Navy. Certainly the Navy needed to put forward the best image of its systems, even if it meant sacrificing one of its own, Captain McVay, to prove that he and *not* the system was at fault.

On taking the witness stand, Commander Hashimoto testified in a confident manner, but respectful of the location and of his hosts/captors. He could not be certain whether or not the target had been zigzagging, but assured the court that this made no difference because he could have struck the ship while she sailed in either mode. His recollection of the conditions of visibility was positive; it was intermittently cloudy and moonlit. The ship was spotted silhouetted against the horizon, but previously it had not been possible to even see the horizon.

The U.S. Navy Public Relations people indicated that the Navy had called Hashimoto not as a witness against Captain McVay but as an expert to establish the cause of the explosion that had sunk the ship. But few believed this. Captain McVay questioned whether or not the witness could be properly sworn — he was not a Christian and could not swear on a Bible, and if he were to assert something or other, who would know if he were being truthful or not? The prosecution asserted that should Hashimoto be found to be lying, he would be turned over to Japanese authorities who would deal sternly with him. (Whatever this meant is not certain, but their answer seemed to satisfy the court.)

In summation, the weight of the testimony of Hashimoto had not favored the prosecution but rather the defendant. But this point didn't really matter, as McVay already had been judged guilty before the trial started, almost reminiscent of Lewis Carroll who wrote, in *Alice in Wonderland*, "Off with his head, the Jury said, this villain must be tried."

The storm over Hashimoto's appearance as a witness continued to rage, with congressmen introducing resolutions calling for his testimony to be stricken from the record. A Louisiana Democrat was the most vociferous in his denunciation of the decision to allow Hashimoto to testify. No points had been scored with the American public. Clearly, if the Navy was fighting for survival, it was doing it in strange ways.

After Hashimoto, there were several other witnesses, principally experts, who only codified how certain actions would obtain certain results, such as "could the ship have floated with one torpedo strike had all watertight doors been closed?"

At this point, the defense had an opportunity to present its case, though it should have known that the jury was no longer out. It appeared from the witnesses called by the defense that its thrust would be to establish that the order to abandon ship had been given promptly; that the result was that more than 900 men had responded and made it safely into the water; and that Hashimoto's statement verified that McVay's ship would not have escaped whether zigzagging or not.

Captain Oliver F. Naquin, a graduate of Annapolis and survivor of the sinking of the submarine USS *Squalus* in 1939, testified as the Operations Officer for the Navy in the Marianas. The prosecution sustained an objection to the question, "Why was the *Indianapolis* allowed to sail without an escort?" But a point was scored when Naquin testified that at the time of sailing there had been only a slight danger of being confronted by enemy submarines.

Captain Alfred N. Granum, Operations Officer of the Philippine Sea Frontier, was the next defense witness, for the purpose of further establishing that the Navy did not believe that enemy submarines were then operating in the area where the *Indianapolis* was sunk. Granum testified that it was the position of the Sea Frontier Command that because many of the reported sightings of enemy submarines had been made by merchant ships and were unsubstantiated, the Command had viewed the likelihood of submarines to be slight. (Granum was reprimanded for not having evaluated properly the potential of enemy submarines in the area where and when the cruiser was sunk. Later, as a result of petitions by Granum and several of the others so chastised, the reprimands were expunged.)

Captain Glynn R. Donaho, of the U.S. Naval Academy, a submariner and Silver Star recipient, testified that he found that zigzagging had no effect on the success of a stalking submarine nor a torpedo attack. Donaho's testimony continued with a sharp and bitter exchange between him and the prosecutor, Captain Ryan, concerning the efficacy of zigzagging. Donaho resorted to the position that naval instructions notwithstanding, he believed that zigzagging would have had no value whatsoever if done PRIOR to the firing of the torpedoes. Ryan tried to shake this testimony, but could get nowhere with Donaho. Publicly there was now spoken a challenge to the time-honored U.S. Navy edict to zigzag when sailing in waters where enemy submarines were present.

At the time that Captain McVay began his defense, a comment appeared in the prestigious *Army-Navy Journal*:

What must have been apparent from the outset to all impartial observers seems now to have become the conviction of the Navy high command — that responsibility for the debacle with its needlessly high toll of American lives must be fixed several echelons higher than a lone commanding officer. For if 800 to 900 men escaped from the sinking ship, as had been testified repeatedly in the proceedings of the court-martial, then the commanding officer of the I-58 accounted for less American lives than did the negligence of the high command. The Navy is instituting preliminary investigations toward fixing responsibility where it properly belongs and if the Navy continues belatedly this forthright approach the public may witness the unusual spectacle of disciplinary action being directed against a three-star naval commander.

It did appear that the plot had thickened. Perhaps even the head of a Flag Officer would fall, as well as that of McVay.

The next day Captain McVay took the witness stand to testify on his own behalf. McVay did indeed stick to the specifics of the charges. His counsel had been coached in the questions that should be asked in order to give McVay the opportunity to tell, in sequence, his story. His telling was consistent with the events as they had been reported by the press before the trial, those spoken during the trial, and indeed, those thereafter. In no instance did McVay contradict what had been said by another witness, and his defense rested on the premise that "having heard from others what I now tell you again it must be clear that I am innocent of the charges."

The testimony of the prosecution and of the defense had been completed and the court, having deliberated, now returned a verdict. To the specification of the first charge, Captain McVay was found guilty; to the specification of the second charge, the court found him not guilty. On the day of the verdict, McVay had learned *only* that he was *not guilty* of the second charge. The *guilty* verdict on charge number one was not read to him at that time. In U.S. Navy regulations, a guilty charge must be made public only after the reviewing authority has approved it. But McVay thought that his Navy career was over.

Captain Ryan, as required by court-martial procedure, entered into the record of the proceedings and also into the personnel record of McVay that the punishment of the court should be that McVay lose 100 numbers in his temporary grade of Captain and 100 numbers in the permanent grade of Commander.

The members of the court, which had just convicted him, all signed a letter to the Reviewing Authority recommending clemency. After the verdict, Admiral Spruance wrote a letter to the Chief of Naval Personnel in which he praised Captain McVay.

McVay's conviction, albeit slight in punishment, did not set well with the public, whose opinion was so important, nor with the press. In editorial after editorial it was written that the U.S. Navy had found a "fall guy" in Captain McVay, that the negligence lay not in events before the sinking as much as those after the sinking, and that the Navy, fighting a serious battle to prevent itself from being unified with the U.S. Army, had selected this scenario as being the one best suited to its needs at the moment.

The verdicts, as regulations required, went upward through the Command so that they might be approved or altered for clemency. James Forrestal, the Secretary of the Navy, on February 20, 1946, declared:

> The proceedings, findings, and sentence are approved. In view, however, of the recommendations of the Chief of Naval Personnel and Fleet Admiral E. J. King, based upon the outstanding record of Captain McVay, which clearly evidences his long and honorable service, performance of duty of the highest order, including combat service in World War II, numerous commendations, and the award of the Expeditionary, China Service, Silver Star and Purple Heart Medals, and further, in view of the unanimous recommendation to clemency signed by all members of the court, the sentence is remitted in its entirety. Captain McVay will be released from arrest and restored to duty.

Captain McVay, having been cleared, was given his next assignment as Chief of Staff of the Eighth Naval District, with headquarters in New Orleans. There he remained until he retired in June 1949, with the rank of Rear Admiral.

In retirement, McVay yet bore the awful memory of the tragedy that had befallen the USS *Indianapolis*. Friends gave him support, and infrequent press and news releases were not unkind. But he was plagued by letters and telephone calls, which continued coming from family members of sailors who had perished in the sinking. He was constantly branded a murderer. Each letter that he would receive might be a denunciation and each telephone call might be a vitriolic tirade accusing him of killing through negligence or indifference. The communications were most numerous on the anniversaries of the sinking.

In a later television report, his son Charles McVay stated that his father was the only person in the entire history of the United States Navy to have been court-martialed for having lost a ship that he commanded. Before McVay, the findings of a Court of Inquiry, though not as severe as a court-martial, had been sufficiently punitive, provided the findings were unfavorable. And such findings meant the end of a career, for the "loss of files" set the officer back in the sequence of promotion seniority, and more so it assured that the officer would never again command a vessel at sea.

Captain McVay lived with the ghosts of the sinking for over 20 years. Finally one sunlit day in 1968, he could take it no longer. He dressed in his Navy uniform and went out into his garden. There, while clutching a Navy doll in his left hand, with his right he placed the muzzle of a Smith & Wesson .38-caliber U.S. Navy revolver in his mouth and fired. He then became the last casualty of the torpedo attack and sinking of the USS *Indianapolis*.

Captain Charles Butler McVay III was an anomaly. The court-martial, which was conducted at the end of World War II, certainly had been staged to show the American public the fairness but sternness of U.S. Navy justice. But, probably, it had the opposite effect. It showed the gross inefficiency of the naval service, which simply could not keep track of its ships.

In the fall of 2000, the U.S. Congress passed a resolution, which President Bill Clinton signed into law, exonerating Captain Charles Butler McVay III and awarding the *Indianapolis* and its crew a Navy Unit Citation. In July 2001, Secretary of the Navy Gordon England ordered a document placed in the Captain's file showing that he had been exonerated. Unfortunately, Captain McVay's son, Kimo Wilder McVay, who had fought to clear his father's name, died two weeks before the file was amended.

Chapter Four

From the Banks
of the Wabash —
the USS *Vincennes*

*V*INCENNES, INDIANA, in southwestern Knox County, is "on the bank of the Wabash" River. The lyrics of the familiar song speak of the Hoosier pride and heart. Vincennes is as truly American as any other city in the country.

In 1936, at the height of President Franklin D. Roosevelt's New Deal, there were but 17,000 living in Vincennes, not too many to keep it from being what was considered "a nice place to live." Winters were mild, summers pleasant, and a thriving chapter of the Ku Klux Klan showed the "old Southern fighting spirit."

Franklin Roosevelt was supported by the state's congressional members. When it came time to take a new U.S. Navy cruiser from the drawing board to the shipyard and to name her, Secretary of the Navy Frank Knox, publisher of the Chicago *Daily News* and Republican stalwart, concurred with the mood to name a ship for the little city on the "banks of the Wabash."

The U.S. Navy has a longstanding practice of naming cruisers after cities, but most were larger and better known than Vincennes — the *Tuscaloosa* (Alabama), *Quincy* (Massachusetts), *San Francisco* (California), and *Wichita* (Kansas). And thus the city of Vincennes was proud when, on January 2, 1934, her keel was laid at the Bethlehem Shipbuilding Company's Fore River plant in Quincy, Massachusetts. Three years and one month later Miss Harriet Virginia Kimball, daughter of the mayor of Vincennes, christened the ship before her launching. Her designation was CA-44 and her first Commander was Captain Burton H. Green.

The *Vincennes* shakedown cruise took her to Stockholm, Sweden; Helsingfors, Finland; La Havre, France; and Portsmouth, England. Later she locked through the Panama Canal to her new posting in Honolulu. The cruiser returned to Mare Island, California, in 1939 for an overhaul, after which she steamed through the Canal to Hampton Roads, Virginia.

After Hitler had invaded Poland, on September 1, 1939, the *Vincennes* went out on "neutrality patrols" in the Atlantic. In 1940, as a diversion from the monotony of patrols, she steamed to Casablanca, French Morocco, where she took on a cargo of gold for transport to the U.S. While she lay at anchor awaiting the delivery of the gold it was learned that Italy, following the example of Germany, had declared war on France, her supposed sister state, on June 10, 1940. The French thought this to be the greatest betrayal. It was the (then) Captain of the *Vincennes,* J. R. Beardall, who reported the ill-feeling toward Italy by the North African French. From the glamour of Casablanca, the *Vincennes* returned to the boredom of Caribbean patrol.

True to the U.S. Navy schedule, she steamed to the Portsmouth Navy Yard, Norfolk, Virginia, for another overhaul in January 1941, and this done, she returned to patrol and convoy duty in the Caribbean and the Atlantic.

As escort to ships laden with British troops in Convoy WAS-12, the *Vincennes* found herself battling heavy seas on December 7, 1941, when radio communication was received of the Japanese attack on Pearl Harbor. The

The USS *Vincennes* at moderate speed in the Pacific Ocean swells.

sea was so rough that a whaleboat and an OS2U float plane had been swept overboard; the crew had little time to speculate on the beginning of the war.

Having safely debarked the British troops in Capetown, South Africa, the ship returned to the Brooklyn Navy Yard to be fitted for war. This done she sailed for the Pacific, via the Canal, in March 1942.

The *Vincennes* became a part of Task Force 18, when she joined the carrier *Hornet* in San Francisco. In her hold were 16 B-25 Mitchell bombers that would carry out the famous "raid on Tokyo" by Colonel James "Jimmy" Doolittle. When in April Japanese trawlers sighted (and reported) the Carrier Force, it was decided to launch the bombers and proceed with the raid immediately. Though the attack was of but minimal success, it had the desired effect — it boosted American morale and deflated that of Japan.

After the aircraft had been launched, the *Vincennes* and the *Hornet* made for Pearl Harbor. After a few days in port she sped toward the war in the Coral Sea. As fate would have it, she arrived too late to participate in the battle. The task force of which the *Vincennes* was a part returned to Pearl.

On May 28, 1942, she departed for the close vicinity of Midway Island, which Intelligence had learned was the next target of Japanese aggression.

On June 4, 1942, the *Vincennes* and the accompanying *Astoria* (CA-34) were north of Midway when Nakajima Navy B5N "Kate" torpedo planes from the carrier *Hiryu* attacked them. The naval escorts began to fire. At 1640 hours, the first air response from the Americans came when a F4F Wildcat off the nearby carrier USS *Yorktown* downed a torpedo plane. As more Kates approached the group and came within range of the *Vincennes's* 5-inch, 20mm, and 1.1-inch antiaircraft guns, the cruiser responded by turning to starboard and increasing her speed to 24 knots. The gunners of the ship brought down a Kate at 150 yards off the port bow — too close for comfort.

The Japanese air attack was short-lived, but long enough to have scored hits severely wounding the *Yorktown*. Her covering ships, the destroyers and the cruisers, began to hover around the stricken carrier, now listing to port, to protect her from further damage. However, their efforts were quite ineffective for in the early hours of June 6, the Japanese submarine I-*168* slipped through the circle of destroyers and torpedoed fatally the *Yorktown* and the destroyer *Hammann* (DD 412), sinking the latter immediately. The carrier managed to stay afloat until the early hours of June 7th when she turned on her side, showed her screws, and sank.

Having lost the ship she had been charged to protect, the *Vincennes* returned to Pearl Harbor for refitting. After spending several days, she was refueled and revictualed and joined the force that was making its way to fight for the Solomon Islands.

The *Vincennes* arrived off Guadalcanal on August 7, 1942 — her "rendezvous with death." At dawn she launched her spotter plane and commenced bombarding the shore to support the invasion. The Marines landed at a lightly defended location. Not until the attackers had penetrated a mile or more into the interior did resistance stiffen — what was to be the most determined Japanese resistance of the Pacific War. At 1320 hours, the Japanese launched a counter-strike attacking the invading landing craft from the air. Being sunward of the Marine transports, the cruiser was in a favorable position to fire upon the attacking Japanese, and she downed two of their planes before they wisely withdrew.

The *Vincennes*, *Quincy*, *Astoria*, and two destroyers, *Jarvis* and *Helm*, patrolled that night but returned to the fray at dawn. The *Vincennes* spent the morning bombarding the coast with no challenge from the Japanese sky. Then at two minutes shy of high noon, Japanese bombers — a total of 27 Mitsubishi G4M "Betty" bombers — swooped down from the sky and, at altitudes of no more than 20 to30 feet above the surface of the sea, attacked the American ships. The destroyer *Jarvis* was the first unlucky one; she took a torpedo that later proved to be enough to sink her.

Later in the afternoon, American spotter planes reported a Japanese surface force, ostensibly three cruisers and three destroyers, coming from the direction of Rabaul. Responding to the impending attack, the *Vincennes*, *Quincy*, and *Astoria* immediately steamed north in that direction to give the Marine transports the greatest protection possible.

The *Vincennes'* Commander, Captain Frederick L. Riefkohl, had been on the bridge continuously since 0445 that morning. At midnight on August 8th, he turned the ship over to his Executive, Commander W. E. A. Mullan, and retired to his cabin to sleep a bit.

Captain F. L. Riefkohl sent the following report to the Commander of Task Force 62 after the sinking of the USS *Vincennes* off Savo Island in the early hours of August 9, 1942.

U.S.S. VINCENNES

CA44/A16-5

Serial No. 0021

14 August 1942

From: Captain F. L. Riefkohl, U.S. Navy,
Commanding Officer, U.S.S. VINCENNES,
Commanding Northeast Screening Group.

To: Commander Task Force 62.

Subject: Report of Action Occurring off Savo Island
(Guadalcanal-Florida Island) Area —
Night of 8/9 August, 1942.

ENCLOSURES: (A) Track Chart (with Part I).
(B) Statements of Officers and Men (with
Part II).

1. This report is submitted in two parts — Part I is a preliminary report, insofar as known covering the operations of the Screening Group. A supplementary report will be submitted on receipt of reports from other vessels of the Group. Part II is a report of VINCENNES activities during the action. All times, bearings, ranges and references to positions or orders are of necessity from memory as no records or notes are available.

PART I

1. AUSTRALIA, VINCENNES and SAN JUAN Groups were assigned night screening sectors by Commander Task Group 62.6 plan of operations. AUSTRALIA Group South of a line bearing 125 degrees true from center of SAVO ISLAND and

extending to the Eastward to longitude 160 degrees, 04 minutes. VINCENNES Group was assigned a sector to the North of the 125 degree line and East of longitude 160 degrees, 04 minutes. Destroyers RALPH TALBOT and BLUE were patrolling on legs of about 6 miles in length to the Northeast and West of SAVO ISLAND, respectively — center of line about 8 miles from SAVO ISLAND.

2. VINCENNES Group, originally consisting of VINCENNES, QUINCY, ASTORIA, JARVIS and HELM was patrolling a five mile square with center at grid position V-77-29. Courses were 315, 045, 155 and 225. Speed 10 knots. The Northwest corner of the square was about 2¾ miles from SAVO ISLAND and Northeast corner about 4 miles from the Easter [*sic*] limit of RALPH TALBOT'S patrol. These courses and positions were selected to insure against possibility of our being mistaken for enemy forces, as might be possible if seen on opposite course by TALBOT or AUSTRALIA Group and to permit checking position by tangents on SAVO, due to reported strong tidal currents. The Easter [*sic*] limit was governed by instructions to remain outside the 100 fathom curve. The grid position of the center of the square, length of sides and axis 315 degrees was reported to the Commanders of AUSTRALIA and SAN JUAN Groups. Information regarding disposition and location of those groups was not received.

3. VINCENNES, QUINCY and ASTORIA were in column in above order. Commanding Officer ASTORIA was in position to lead the column in case it was desired to reverse course by ship movements. JARVIS and HELM were assigned A/S [*antisubmarine*] screening stations on starboard and port bow, respectively due to enemy submarines operating in the area. All ships of Group were ordered to man Radars. Doctrine for night attacks, including support and concentration of striking group destroyers of screening force had been prescribed by Commander Task Group 62.6.

4. During the heavy torpedo and bombing attack 8 August JARVIS was hit by a torpedo. A replacement was requested of Commander Task Group 62.6. WILSON was ordered and joined up about 2300 taking A/S screening station on the starboard bow.

5. During the afternoon of 8 August a report was received that 3 enemy cruisers, 3 DD's [*destroyers*] and 2 PG's [*patrol gunboats*] or AV's [*seaplane tenders*] had been sighted at 1025 Zone-11 time on course 120 degrees (t), speed 15. The reported position was about 300 miles, to the Northwest of our position. Another report apparently on the same force reported 2 CA's 1 CL one ship of SOUTHAMPTON class, some DD's (number not remembered) and some unidentified at about 1200 (Zone-11) about 25 miles south of the first position. It was assumed that this group was escorting the AV's to some base where planes would be unloaded and be ready to attack us at dawn. The cruisers and DD's could then proceed at high speed and attack our force some time during the mid watch. Note was made of this in my NIGHT ORDERS and importance of being particularly on the alert was stressed.

6. At about 2350 (Z-11) RALPH TALBOT (JIMMY) sent out a report by TBS, that he had seen an airplane with running lights standing toward the Transport Area. At this time fire on GEO. F. ELLIOTT was burning brightly and the glow from the fire near TULAGI was clearly visible.

7. At midnight the Executive Officer, Commander W.E.A. Mullan, U.S.N., was on the bridge to relieve me. Lieutenant Commander C.D. Miller, U.S.N., relieved the Navigator, Commander A.M. Loker, U.S.N., as Officer of the Deck. At about 0050 considering it necessary to get some rest I returned to the emergency cabin adjoining the pilot house, having given my NIGHT ORDERS to the Executive Officer and the Officer of the Deck. At 0120 change of course to 315° was ordered and at 0200 to course 045°. Ship was in condition of readiness II with

2 guns manned in each turret and all loaded. AA battery fully manned.

8.   At about 0145 the Officer of the Deck called me and reported star shell and some firing on our port hand. Being fully clothed I immediately went into the pilot house. The general alarm was sounded. The Executive Officer reported seeing some firing and silhouettes of ships which he recognized as cruisers of our AUSTRALIA Group. The ship was about 3.5 miles West of SAVO ISLAND. I observed 3 or 4 star shell about on the Port beam at a considerable distance and a ship firing star shell toward the Southeast. Some ship about 30° to the left was firing toward the first ship. I saw no ships and no heavy gun fire or searchlights. I estimated that AUSTRALIA Group had made a contact with a destroyer. I received no report of the contact or orders to concentrate. I thought this contact probably a destroyer and a ruse to draw off my Group while the main attack force passed through my sector to attack the Transports. If enemy heavy ships had been sighted I expected AUSTRALIA Group would illuminate and engage them, and the situation would soon be clarified. I considered turning right to course 045°(t), but I felt I might be called on to support AUSTRALIA Group. I signaled speed 15 knots to the Group and decided to hold my course temporarily. Fired no star shell as I did not wish to disclose myself to an enemy approaching my sector from seaward. Took a look on Starboard hand but saw nothing. TBS signal for increased speed had just been sent, when about 0150, three searchlights bearing around 205° were seen and soon were on us. I ordered Group to fire on opportune targets. I had seen no ships and none had been reported other than AUSTRALIA Group. I particularly wanted to guard against firing on friendly vessels, but had to fire on searchlights. After action, Gunnery Officer reported seeing star shell bearing about 180° distance about 10 miles, at about 0145.

9.   VINCENNES turrets fired on right hand searchlight and broadside 5" fired star shell, but not before enemy had fired and

hit her with 8" and 5" projectiles. After the second salvo search-light went out and an explosion was observed on target. Speed was increased to 20 knots and a turn made to the left with a view of closing the enemy and continuing around on a reverse course if he stood in toward the Transport area. Attempts to signal increase in speed failed due to loss of intership communication facilities after the bridge was hit. I intended to make my turns by simultaneous ship turns but could not do so as I was unable to send any signals. One five inch shell of the first salvo that hit us struck the port forward side of the bridge killing the Communication Officer. Fragments entered the pilot house killing or seriously wounding several men.

10. The ship had turned and was on course, 275°(t) when, due to being constantly hit, I swung to the right in hopes of throwing off enemy fire to some extent, and rang up flank speed 25 knots. Other turns to left and right were ordered, but were not effective. The speed signal was not answered and all efforts to communicate with the engineroom or central were fruitless. All interior communication facilities in the pilot house failed after the first or second hit except the ship service telephone. When called on this line no reply was received from Engineroom, Central or Main Battery Control. QUINCY was observed on fire aft, on our port hand. ASTORIA was not seen. HELM and WILSON were ahead and on starboard hand until we turned right. One destroyer was then observed crossing our bow from port to starboard while the other was crossing from starboard to port. The one crossing from port to starboard may have been an enemy, but as the two vessels barely missed colliding and did not fire on one another it is believed that they were both friendly. One DD, on our starboard hand, probably WILSON was observed firing star shell and what appeared as heavy A/A [*antiaircraft*] machine gun fire.

11. The enemy was not illuminated and was not seen at any time except indistinctly by the Gunnery Officer, at about 0200 when he appeared to be on course about 115°(t). No report was

made to Conn that enemy ships were seen at any time. The only points of aim available were enemy searchlights which were on for a short time when they commenced firing and some time later on our starboard hand as enemy was standing out. Fires which were started on VINCENNES first in the hangar, on planes on catapults, signal flags in bags and about the decks made it unnecessary for enemy to use searchlights. Counter illumination was not attempted as enemy searchlight was believed to be on a Destroyer, and illumination of enemy by our DD's was expected.

12. About 0208 ship had swung to a heading about 340° — two destroyers illuminated her from bearings about 120° and 150° relative. Ship was being repeatedly hit by 8" and 5" shells on starboard side but had no guns that could fire and could not make smoke to cover herself. Messengers were sent to Main Battery control, Central and Engineroom asking for gunfire on DD searchlights and to ascertain the situation in Central and Engineroom. My first impression was that these DD's might be our own as the bearing changed very slowly. We must have been swinging left at the time!

13. At least two and possibly four torpedo hits were received on the port side. At about 0213 the enemy searchlights were turned off and firing ceased shortly thereafter. As the ship was listing badly life rafts were ordered put over and word passed to stand by to abandon ship. At about 0230 when the list had increased and it was apparent that ship could not remain afloat I gave the order to abandon ship, which was carried out in a quiet and orderly manner. The wounded were fitted with life jackets and assisted by their shipmates. At about 0240 I left the bridge with my Chief Yeoman, L. E. Stucker, U.S.N., (JA Talker), and my Orderly Corporal J. L. Patrick, U.S.M.C., and went down to the upper deck to expedite the crew abandoning ship as I realized the ship would soon go over. I passed the word along for all remaining personnel to get off immediately. As the water reached the part of the deck where I was standing I started

swimming and was just clear of the mast when it hit the water. The ship sank at about 0250. Rescue was started by Destroyers about 0615. The personnel on my raft were recovered about 0820.

14. It is believed that the enemy entered from the Westward of Savo Island and close by the Island where clouds are usually hanging and visibility is bad. He probably first observed our Group to the Eastward silhouetted by the glow of a fire on Tulagi, and later to the North Eastward in which direction due to low lying Islets I had noted the visibility was quite good. I saw nothing of the enemy except searchlights. It is believed that he passed under our stern and went out to the Northward of us about 0210 while we were illuminated and he was firing on our Starboard hand.

15. An accurate estimate of shell hits received is not obtainable but it is believed that between seventy-five and one hundred shells hit. There were 8", 4".7 and (or) 5".5. Three or four torpedo hits were received on the port side. Airplanes were reported overhead. I cannot tell whether or not bombs were dropped. Submarines were in the vicinity. One on the surface is reported to have been fired on and a hit registered at the base of the conning tower.

16. I have not yet received reports from other vessels in VINCENNES Group.

17. Part II covering more detailed report of VINCENNES operations during the action will be submitted as soon as necessary data can be obtained.

F. L. RIEFKOHL

From the reports by Captain Riefkohl and other crew members, it was verified that less than an hour after Riefkohl took to his bed for rest to be fresh for the morning's battle, he had been awakened with news that the ship had been illuminated by star shells. The Japanese had chosen not to wait until daylight to begin their mischief. Hardly had he gotten to the bridge when his ship and the others of his Group (*Quincy*, *Astoria*, *Jarvis*, and *Helm*) were in the glare of Japanese searchlights and then fired upon with five- and eight-inch shells. The *Vincennes* responded, trying to blow out the offending lights, but before she could do so she was hit by several salvos, which knocked out the bridge to engine-room communications. As it became apparent that to get away was the better part of valor, she had attempted to increase speed and alter course, but to no avail.

At 0200 hours she had been hit by several Japanese torpedoes, which put the number one fireroom out of action and holed her bottom so badly that she began to list. Soon she was dead in the water and the Japanese lost interest, concentrating their attention on the ships that yet lived and yet fought.

Shortly after the Japanese stopped the shelling, Riefkohl ordered that the ship be abandoned, which began immediately. The Captain was the last to leave at 0240. The lifeboat to which he swam was picked up after daylight, about 0800.

Forty-five of 68 officers and 681 of the 1,003 sailors had survived — an almost identical casualty ratio.

In less than an hour, the Japanese had sunk the *Vincennes*, *Quincy*, *Astoria*, and HMAS [*His Majesty's Australian Ship*] *Canberra*, without a single loss of Japanese life. The enemy then leisurely sailed away.

Admiral A. J. Hepburn, USN (Ret.), was called to conduct the investigation into the action and the sinking, because of his exemplary career including that of Commander of the U.S. Fleet.

Admiral Hepburn concluded that surprise was the immediate cause of the defeat. However, the underlying cause was the lack of battle experience on the part of the Commanders of two groups of the Task Force, Captain Bode of the USS *Chicago* of the Northern Group and Captain Riefkohl of the USS *Vincennes* of the Southern Group. Although Riefkohl lost his ship, Bode retained his and his Command.

At the end of 1942, Captain Bode returned to the United States and was assigned to Command the Naval Station at Balboa, in the Canal Zone.

Both Bode and the cruiser *Chicago* were destined for death. Having survived the ordeal of the *Vincennes* inquiry, Bode returned to Balboa and after a few days took his own life with his .45-caliber automatic while in the bathroom of his quarters. The USS *Chicago*, damaged by torpedoes in the August 1942 Savo Island engagement, had returned to the States for repairs. She subsequently returned to the Pacific and was sunk at the Battle of Rennell Island in the Solomons on January 29, 1943.

Captain Riefkohl, loquacious and affable, put up a good front, though he knew that the star he had been promised when his command of the *Vincennes* would be over would never become his. His assignment, after the debacle at Savo was that of Liaison Officer with the Mexicans at Vera Cruz, where the Gulf Sea Command practiced war exercises.

To America, the defeat at Savo Island was devastating. Pearl Harbor had been "unsporting" of the Japanese, but at Savo we had had fair warning and had been beaten by an enemy force two-thirds the strength of ours. Melvin Maas, the Minnesota Republican from Congress and a U.S. Marine Reserve Colonel, wrote in the 1943 *Congressional Record*:

> As to the Solomons I have already indicated the confusion and lack of co-ordination in the initial stages. The later engagement in which we lost four heavy cruisers can be charged to negligence and to divided responsibility. Our force was warned during the afternoon that three Jap cruisers were approaching at a speed of 15 knots. Our commander did not believe the three enemy warships would dare attack our much larger force and even if they dared, they would not come within range until the following morning. But the Japs increased their speed, executed a daring maneuver, and within eight minutes our four cruisers had been hit mortally and the attackers were gone.
>
> Now why do I insist that this tragic mistake be recognized, since it cannot be undone? Because an effort had been made to "alibi" this disaster. We have been told that it was necessary to sacrifice these ships in order to protect our transports; that by resisting the Japs these ships saved our landing party from attack. None of this is true. Because the Japs were so heavily

outnumbered, they obviously had no intention of pressing the attack and reaching our transports. They planned a hit-and-run engagement and they pulled it off. I believe it is safer for us to admit this and be on guard against recurrence than to pretend that we were not asleep.

Epilogue

*B*E NOT SURPRISED! This is the hallmark of both the U.S. Navy and the U.S. Army. To win is the expected; to lose is the possible. But to be surprised and, thus, to lose is unacceptable. Within both services are numerous means of warning available to Commanders to prevent impending disaster.

The front-line Army Commander has "eyes and ears," through his subordinates, extending to his immediate front and flanks. Although the possible actions of "deep-placed" enemy artillery are not known, the Army Commander *does know* that all hell may fall on his position at any time. To forestall devastating effects, he digs in and is ready for the moment when the enemy artillery lifts and enemy ground troops begin to pour toward his lines. Albeit he may be overwhelmed, at least he had warning.

The combat Navy Commander has as his "eyes and ears" only the information sent to him through friendly communication channels and those meager facilities within his ship. He must "keep-up, maneuver when commanded to do so, fire on order or not on order, be always alert, and respond to whatever comes with the proper display of the capabilities of the ship." Every second, every minute, in the life and actions of a ship are critical to the outcome. There is no forgiveness at sea.

This book speaks to Navy Commanders who were surprised. Captain F. L. Riefkohl, Commander of the USS *Vincennes*, had been surprised by the sudden appearance of an undetected Japanese Task Force, which put his cruiser out of action with repeated salvos of eight- and five-inch shells, and by submarines that crept in and torpedoed the stricken ship. No cruiser should be put out of action with eight- and five-inch shells.

Lieutenant Commander William J. Tierney had been surprised when his left turn of the USS *Hobson* brought her under the bow of the carrier USS *Wasp* and his ship was cut in half.

Commander Edward A. Broadwell of the USS *Bache* had been surprised when the rocks in the harbor of Rhodes rose up to hole him.

Where no enemy was expected, Captain Charles B. McVay III of the USS *Indianapolis* had been surprised when, while in his well-won sleep, a Japanese torpedo struck his ship.

In truth, no one was more surprised than these four Commanders. In sum, a total of more than 80 years of U.S. Navy training had gone into preparation for their fateful moment when they were overtaken. Their stories were no different from the hundreds of Navy ship Commanders who likewise had been met with the unexpected, but had survived.

Chance, luck, fate, alertness. Which of these spelled the doom of these ships? In the Aleutians, the gallant little USS *Bache* had turned into the path of a Japanese cruiser, and, with her guns blazing, persuaded the enemy to turn back and quit the battle. All of the ships written about had sustained kamikaze attacks or the fire from Nazi shore batteries and had survived.

Perhaps it is the Commander that makes the difference. So many options are open to a U.S. Navy Commander confronted with an impending threat. True, he cannot summarily turn tail and run, but neither can the ground Commander. Most often the ground Commander has time on his side — but not so on the open sea.

For the military Commander, be it at sea or on land, the sanguine philosophy of Karl von Clausewitz must be foremost in mind. In his 1831 classic *On War,* he wrote: "He who neglects the possible in quest of the impossible is a fool." Each of the four Commanders had neglected the possible. Each had lost his ship — chance, luck, fate, alertness notwithstanding!

Bibliography

Bauer, Lieutenant Colonel Eddy. *The History of World War II.* New York: Galahad Press, 1979.

Cincinnati Post and Star Times, February 7, 1968, 15A.

Communication from Chief Petty Officer Walter Frisbee to Vance Rankin.

Communication with Vance Rankin, Esquire.

Dictionary of American Naval Fighting Ships. Washington, D.C.: Government Printing Office, Naval Historical Center, 1991.

Encyclopedia Britannica, 1957, Rhodes, Greece.

Janes Fighting Ships, Janes Yearbooks. London: Paulton House, Shepardess Way, 1972.

National Geographic, August 1972.

Naval Research Section (NRS) 211, NRS 1973-96, NRS 1979-58, NRS 1971-17, NRS 1980-6. Washington, D.C.: Library of Congress.

Newcomb, Richard F. *Abandon Ship, Death of the USS* **Indianapolis**. New York: Holt, Rinehart and Winston, 1958.

_____, *Savo: The Incredible Naval Debacle Off Guadalcanal*. New York: Holt, Rinehart and Winston, 1961.

Parrish, Thomas, ed. *The Simon and Schuster Encyclopedia of World War II*. New York: Simon and Schuster, 1978.

Persons, Benjamin S. *Relieved of Command*. Manhattan, KS: Sunflower University Press, 1997.

Record of Court of Inquiry — Collision of USS *Wasp* and USS *Hobson*, 1952. Washington, D.C.: U.S. Navy Archives.

Record of Court of Inquiry into Circumstances Attendant with Grounding of USS *Bache* at Rhodes, Greece, February 6, 1968. Washington, D.C.: U.S. Navy Archives.

Record of Court of Inquiry into the sinking of the USS *Indianapolis*, 1945. Washington, D.C.: U.S. Navy Archives.

Record of Court of Inquiry into the sinking of the USS *Vincennes*, August 1942. Washington, D.C.: U.S. Navy Archives.

Stanton, Doug. *In Harm's Way: The Sinking of the USS Indianapolis and the Extraordinary Story of Its Survivors*. New York: Henry Holt & Company, 2001.

U.S. Navy Archives photographs, Washington, D.C.

USS **Indianapolis***: Lost at Sea*, Discovery Channel, April 27, 1999.

USS *Vincennes* Action Report, U.S. Navy Serial 0021, August 14, 1942. Washington, D.C.: U.S. Navy Archives.

Whitley, M. J. *Destroyers of World War Two: An International Encyclopedia*. Annapolis: MD: Naval Institute Press, 1988.

Index

by Lori L. Daniel